Cat Cafe Drawings

Drawings and Story
By

Hugh McMahon

With

Rose Earhart and Roberto A. Alfalla

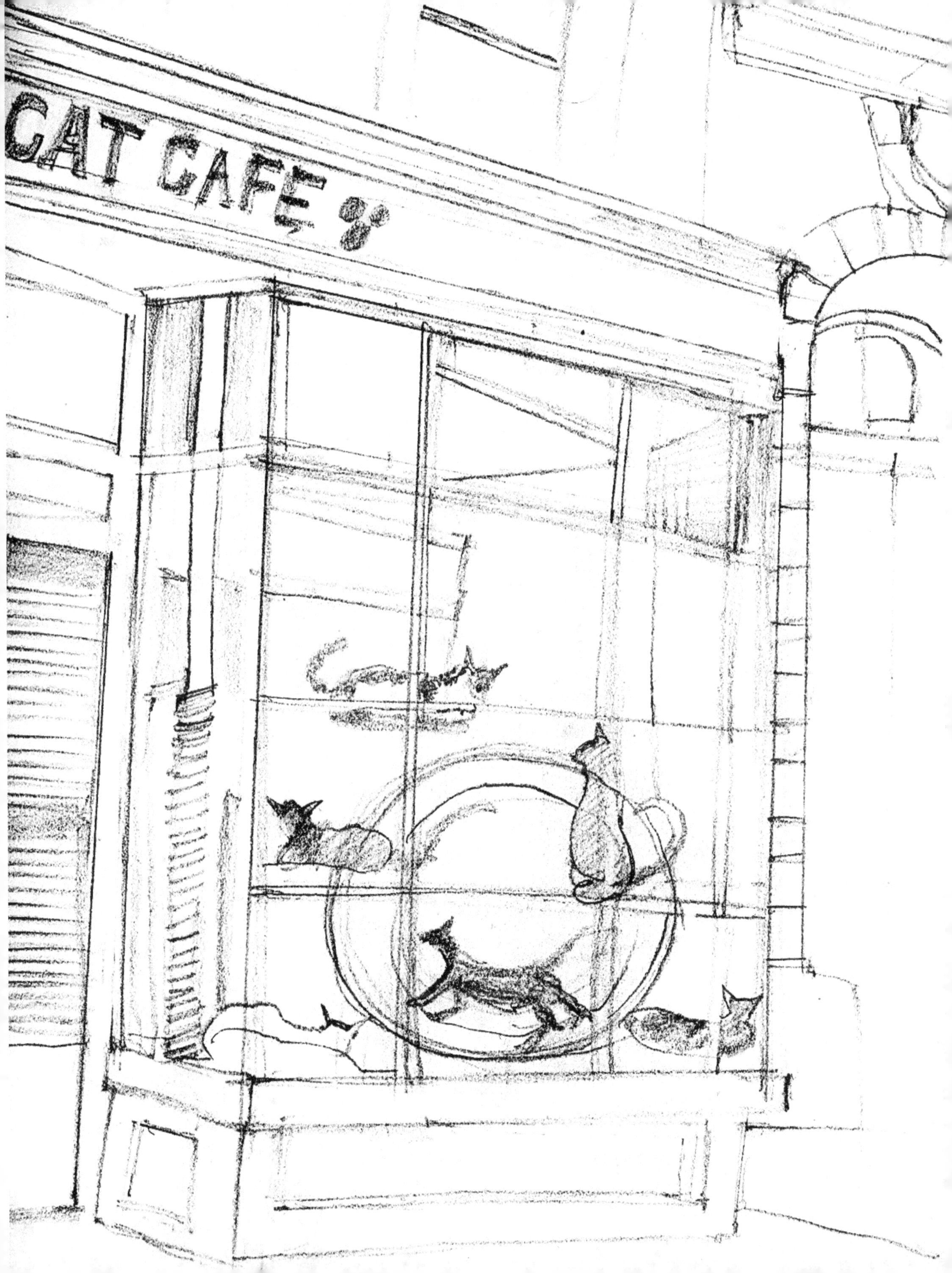
CAT CAFE

Ancient Instinct compels cats to
drink from running water, knowing
that germs multiply in puddled still
water.

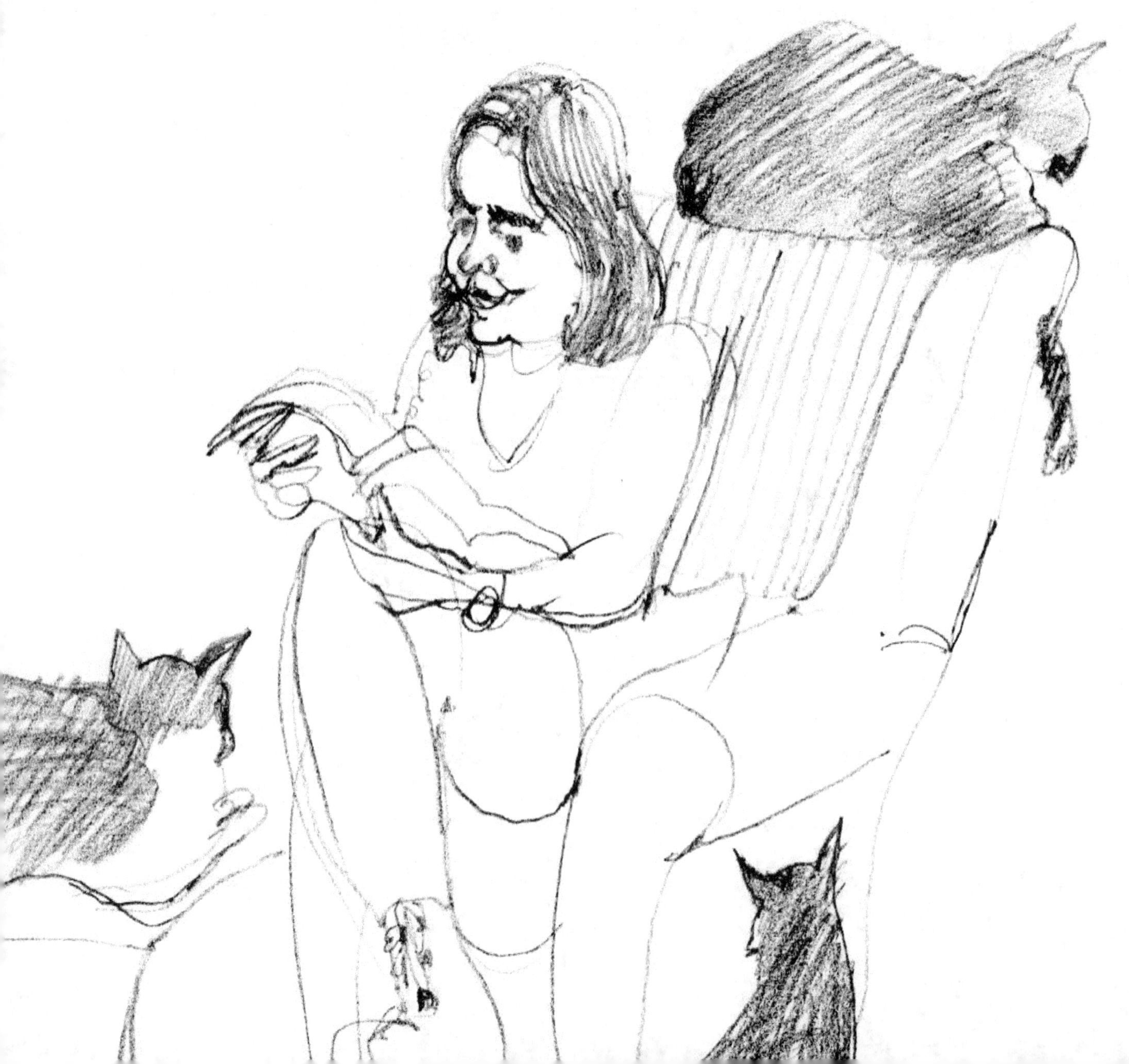

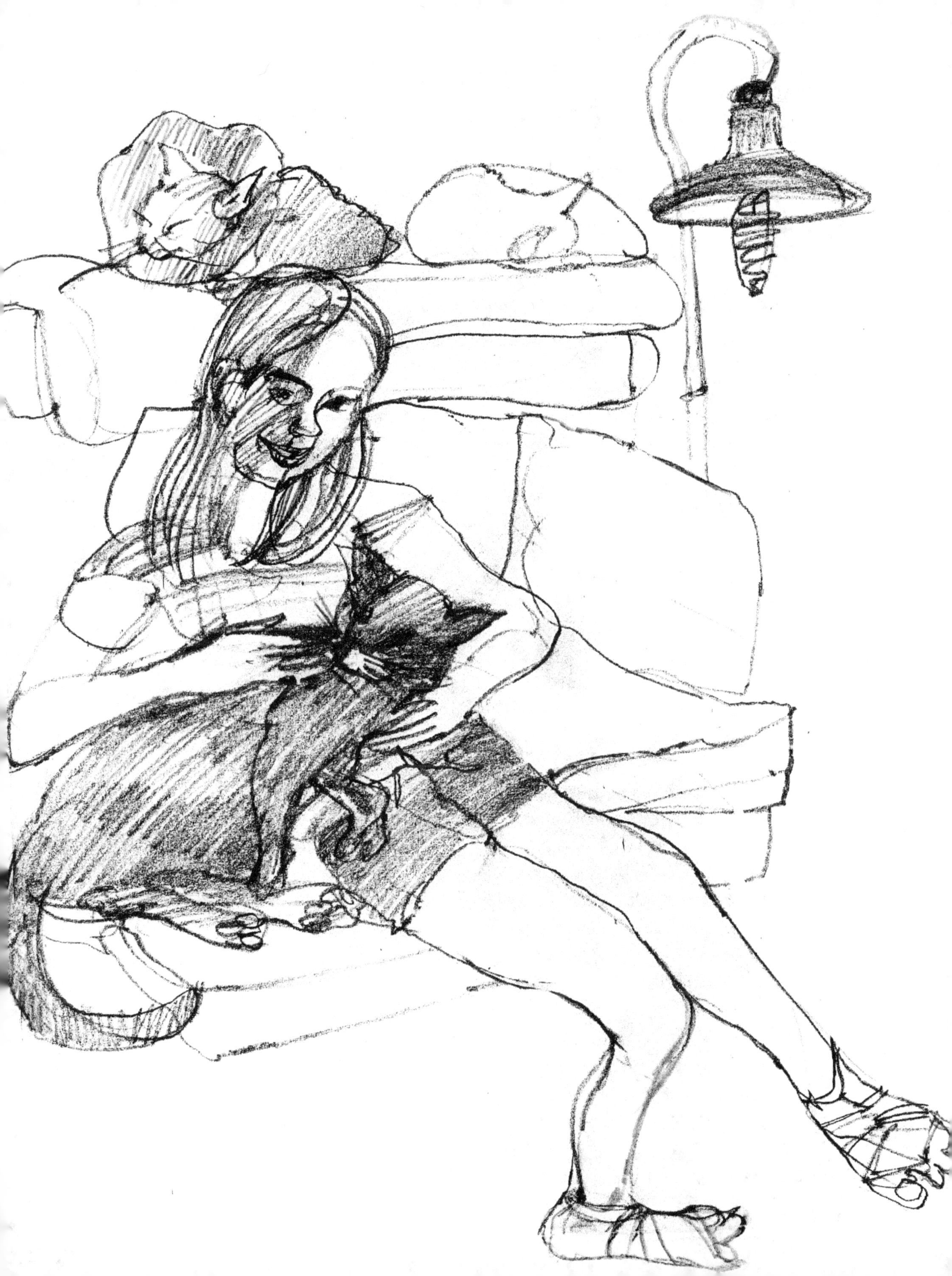

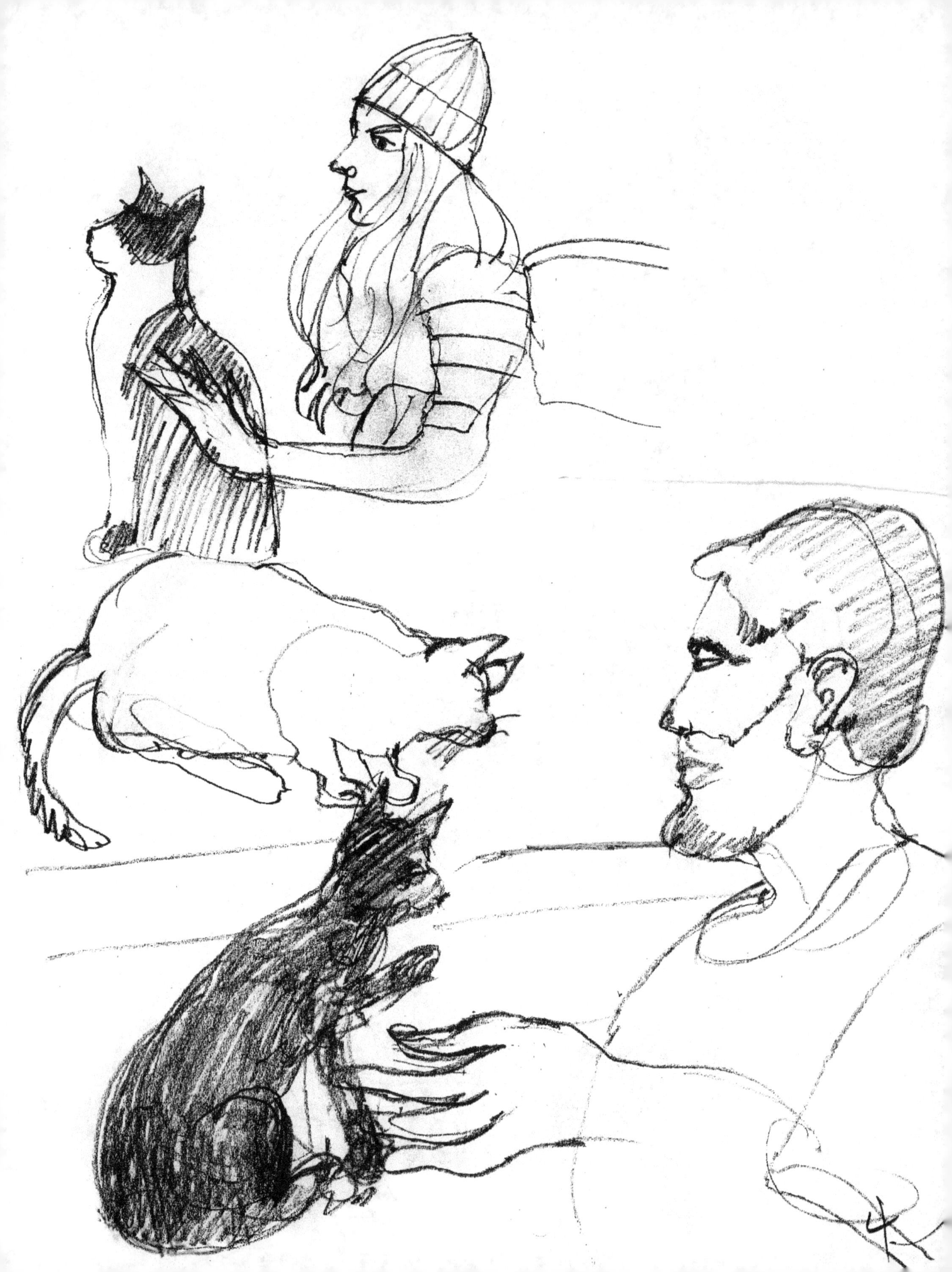

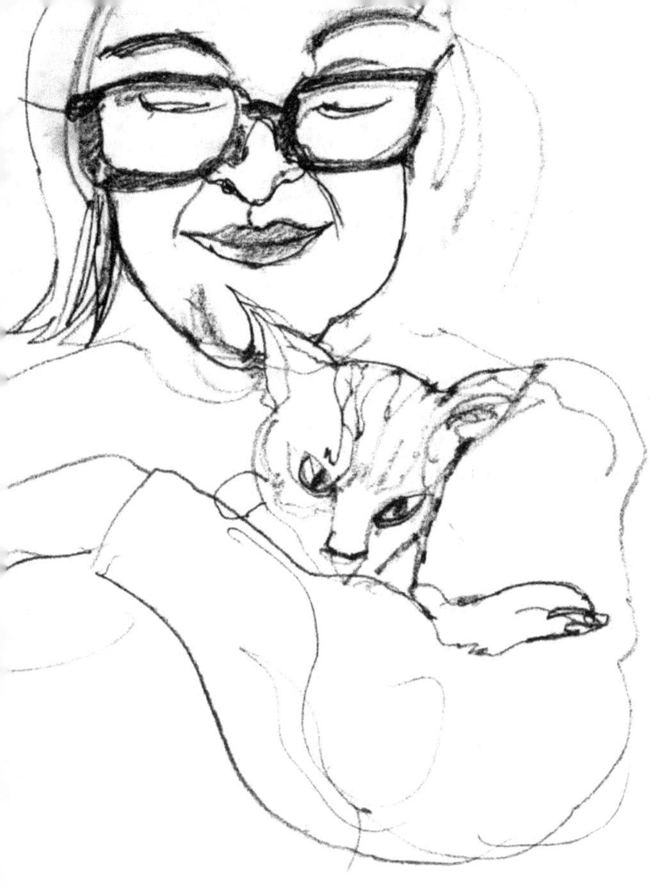

"Cat Flower Garden" was the name of the first Cat Café in the late 1990's, Taipei, Taiwan.

A Cat café is an adoption rescue center where people sample a cat's affections before choosing to take it home or not.

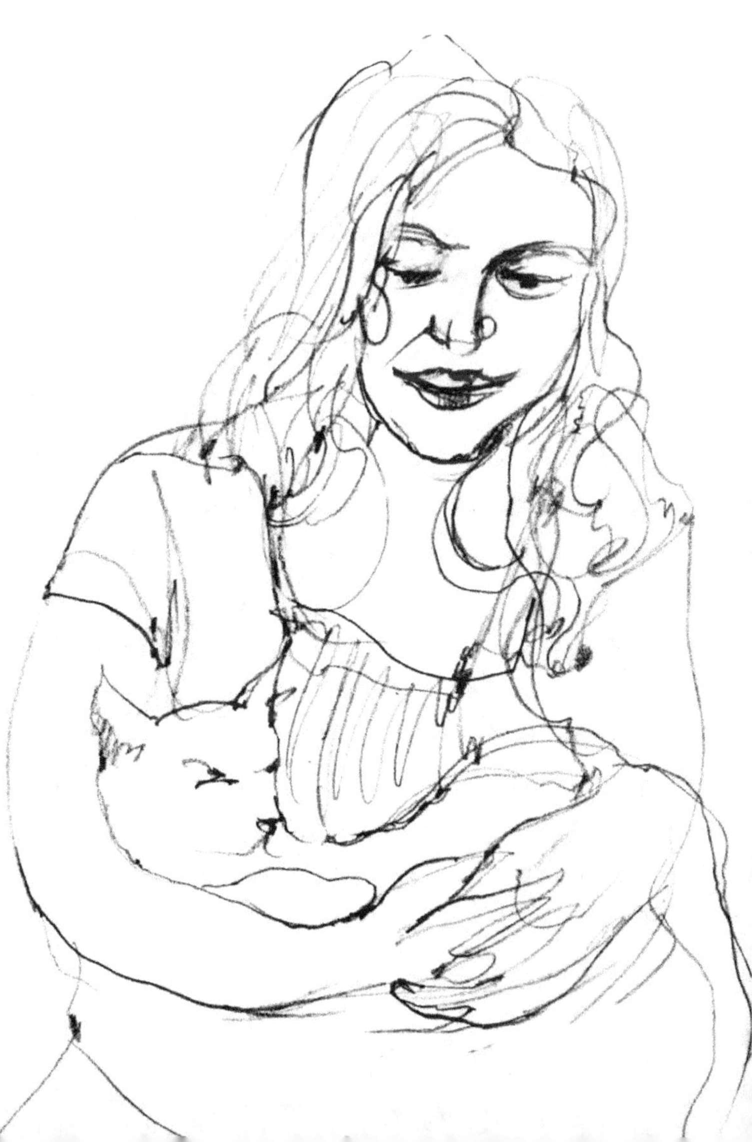

Feral cats are stray roaming cats that lack the ability to relate to human affections. Some live in cat packs and practice allomothering, where the roll of the mother is practiced by the group.

Allogrooming means cats perform special grooming as a group.

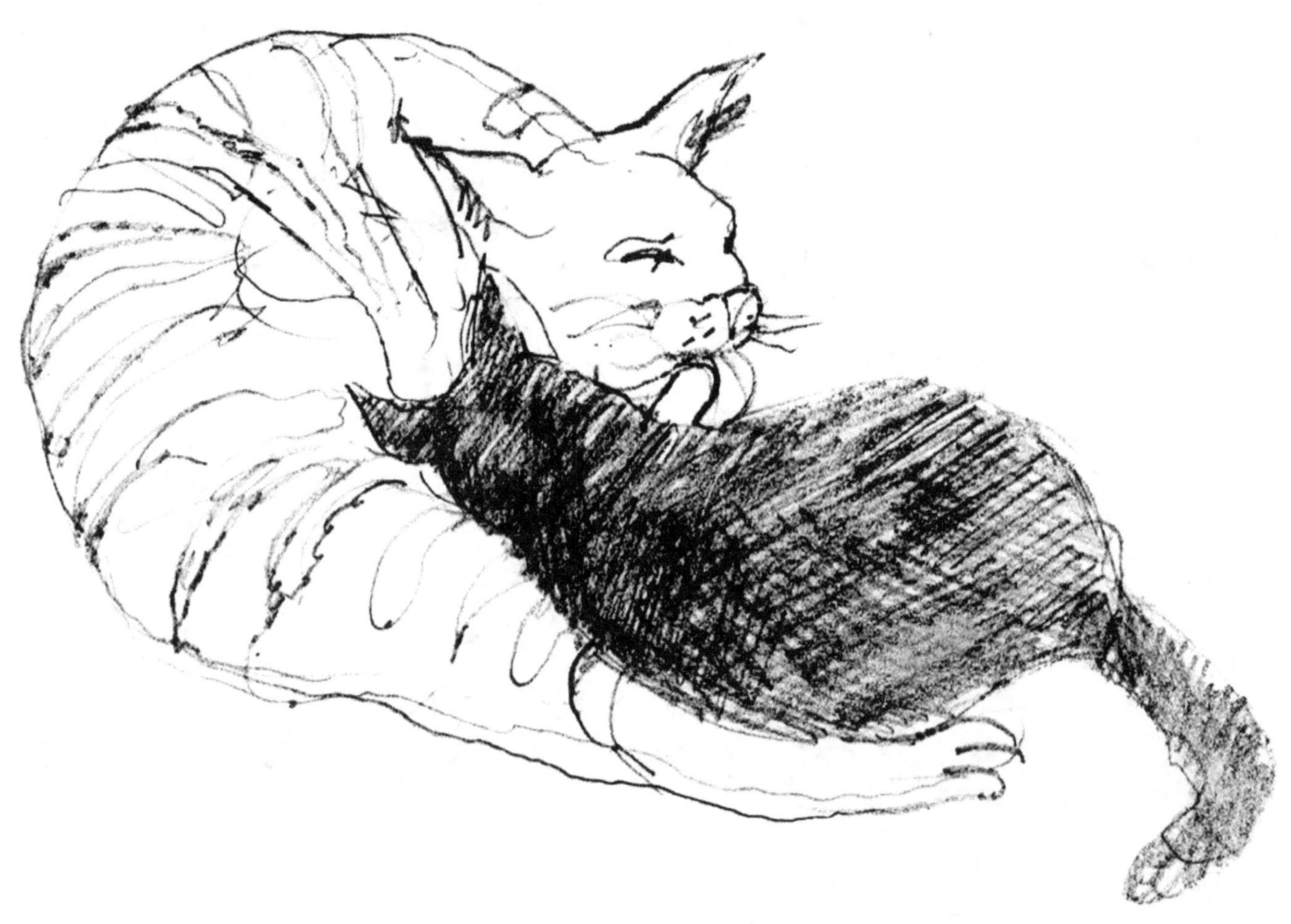

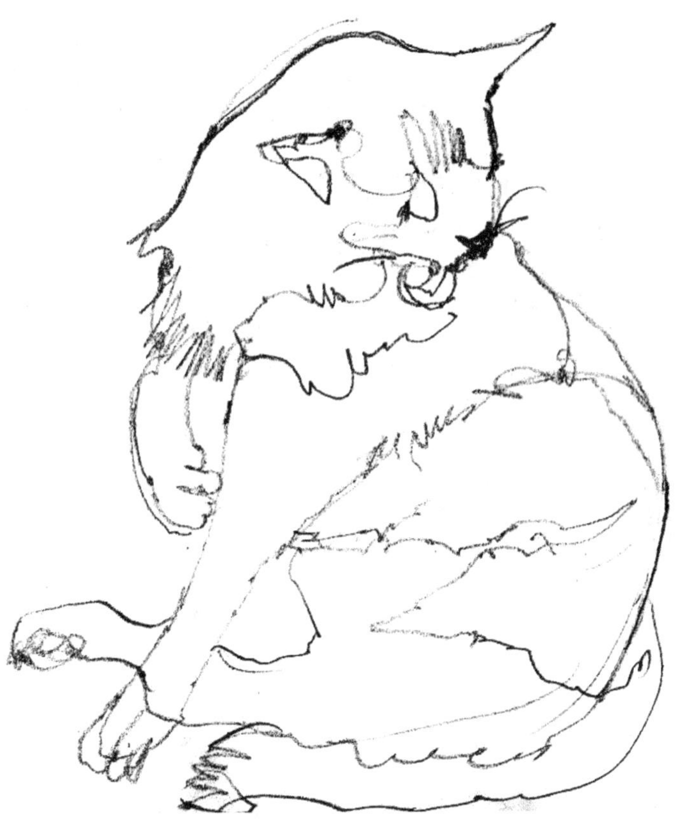

A group of cats is a "clowder" A "kindle" is a group of kittens. An upchucked hairball is a "bezoar."

The cats tongue has a rough texture called hooked "papilla" that helps clean off the bones of prey and enhance grooming.

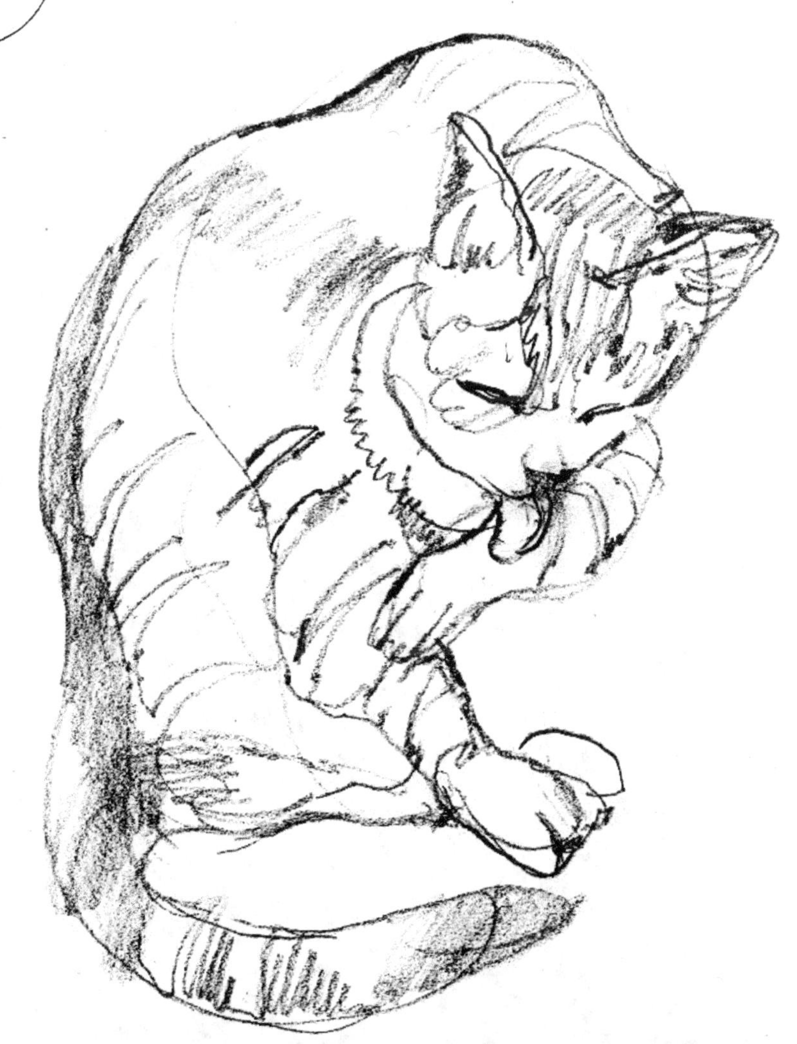

Pest control was the catalyst for transition of wild cats into human civilization. As protectors of crops from destructive rodents.

Felis Silvestra Lybica (Wild Cats)
Felis Catus (Domestic Cats)

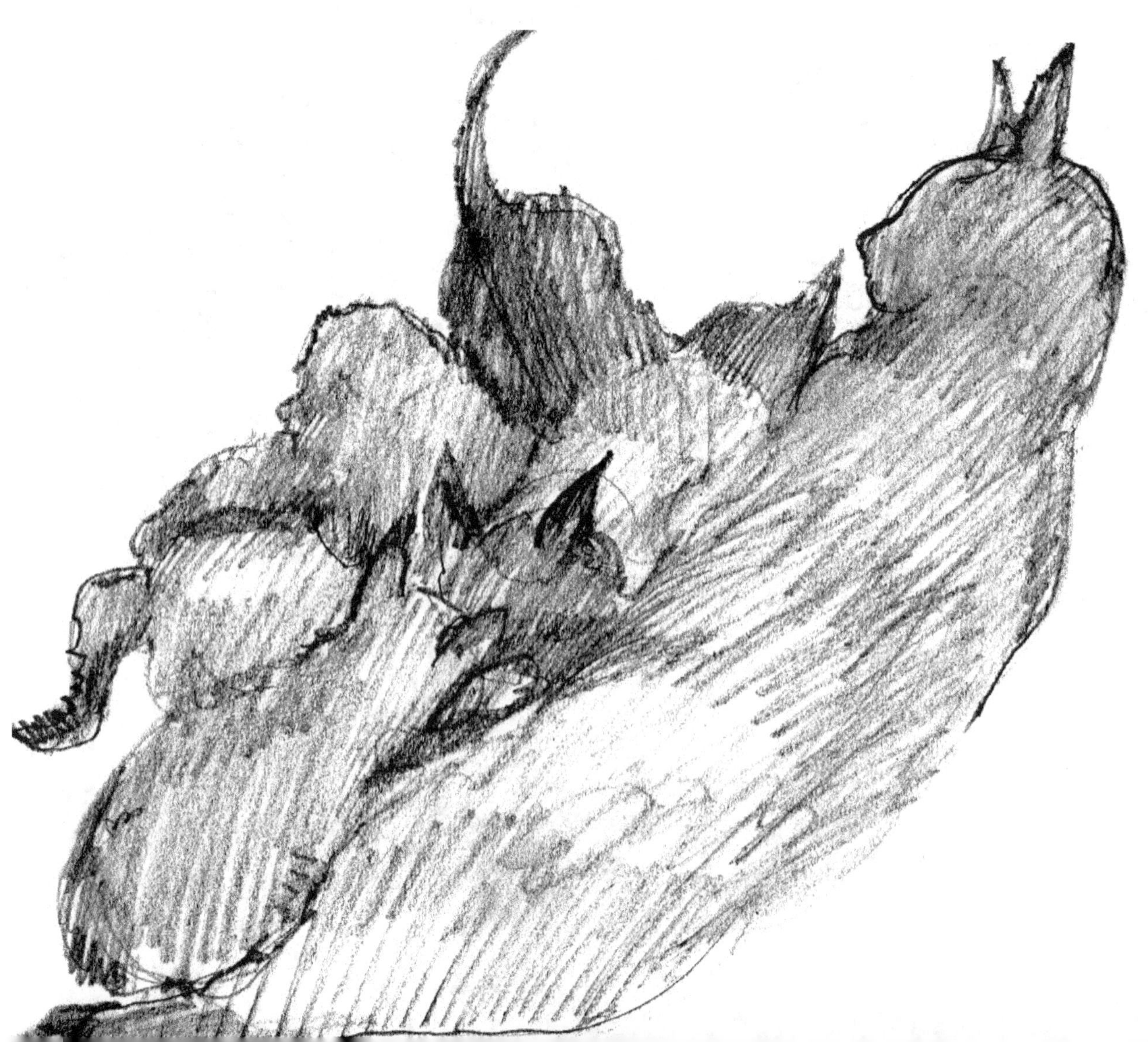

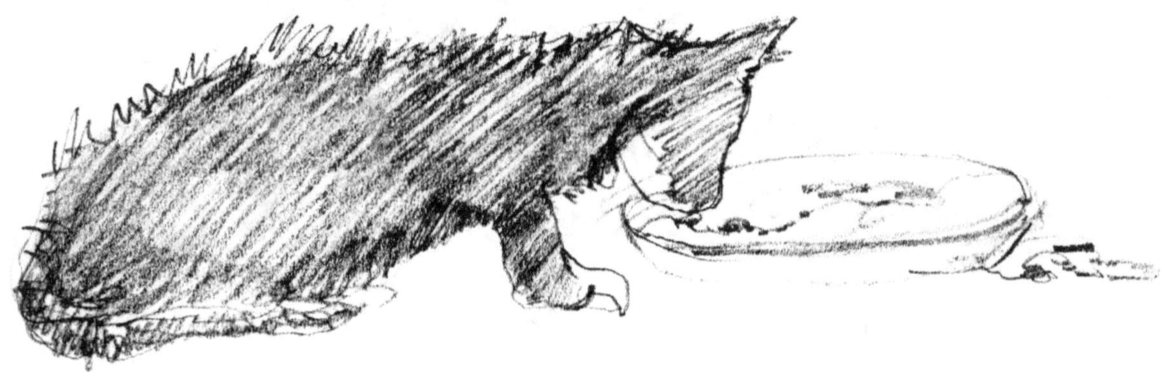

Cats and human have been living side by side for over 9,000 years. Cat and Human bones were found in Neolithic graves.

The Fertile Crescent of Egypt was one of the first sanctuaries for wild cats. Domestication of cats started to crop up in Egyptian art 4,000 years ago. The Goddess Bastet depicted as protector of home, cats, and perfumes. The cat rose to deity status and the punishment for killing a cat was death.

The Egyptian "Mau" is the oldest known breed of domestic cat. The Egyptian word for cat is "Mau.

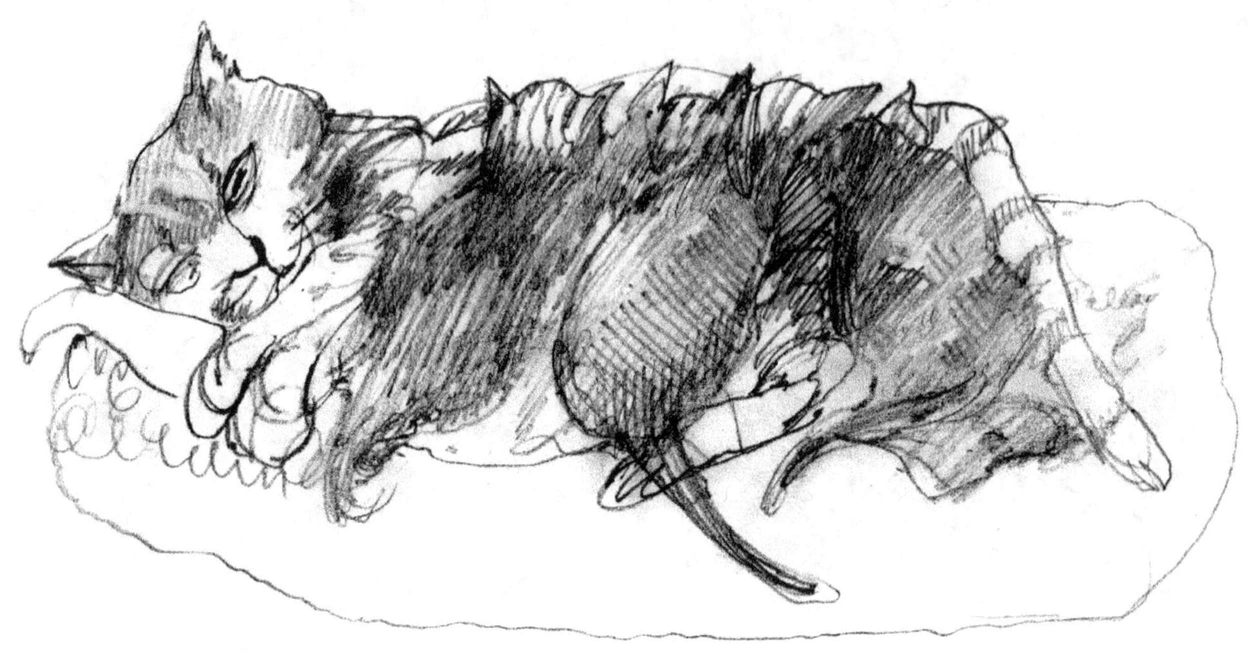

Bastet was the daughter of the
Sun God Ra, goddess of fertility and embodied the
soul of Isis. She was visually represented as being
among kittens.

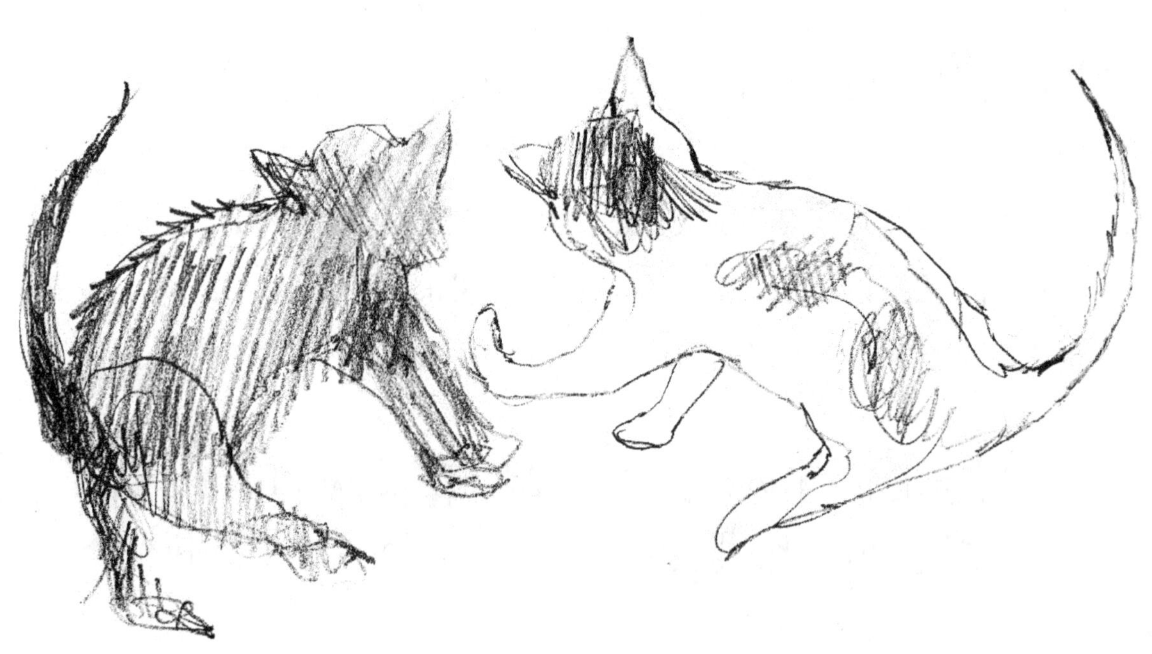

This Egyptian worship honored the cat with the sacred ceremony of mummification . Mummified cats and kittens were embalmed in the catacombs of their Masters. Mummified mice shared this entombment.

Most of a kitten's growth takes place during sleep.

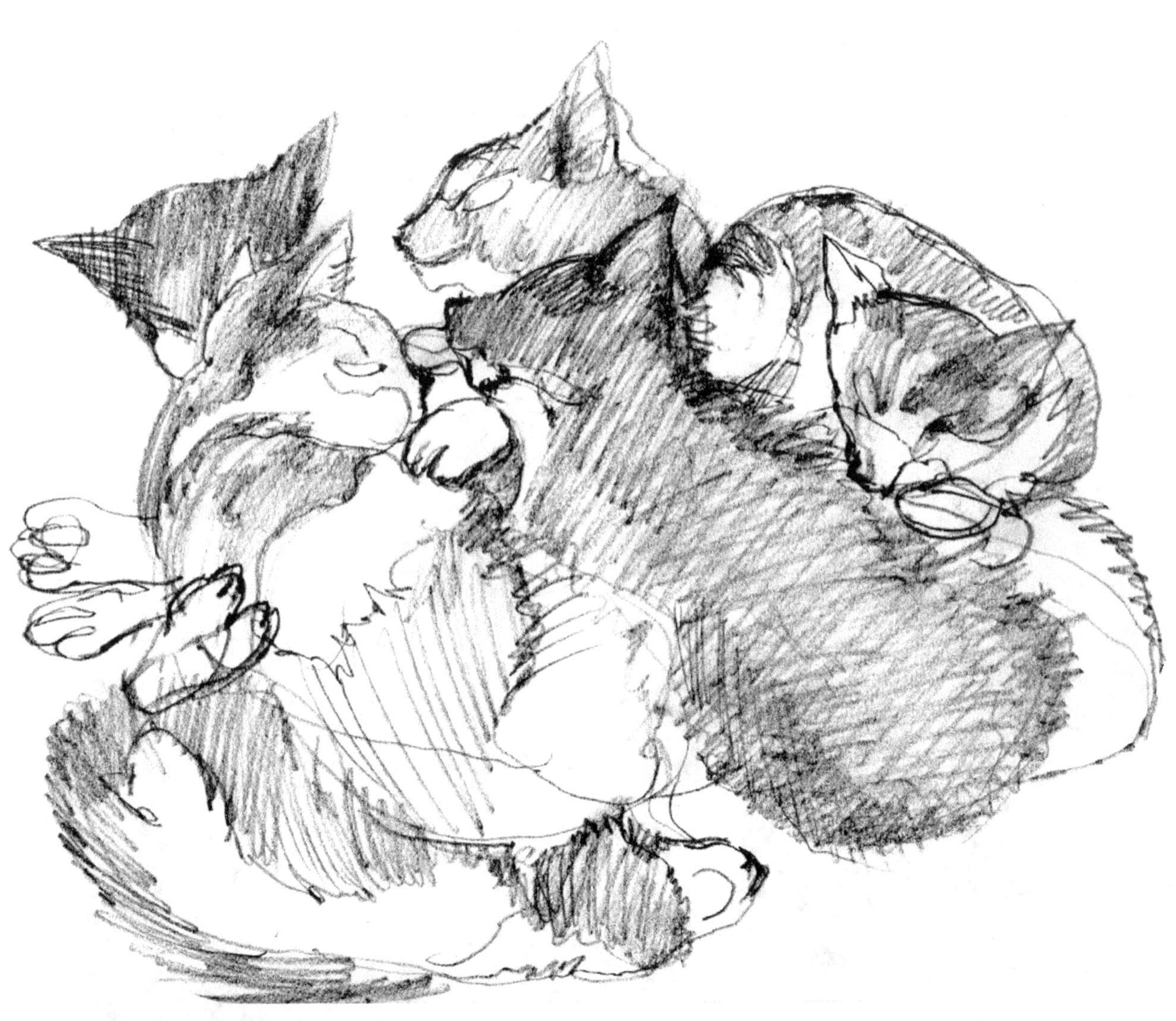

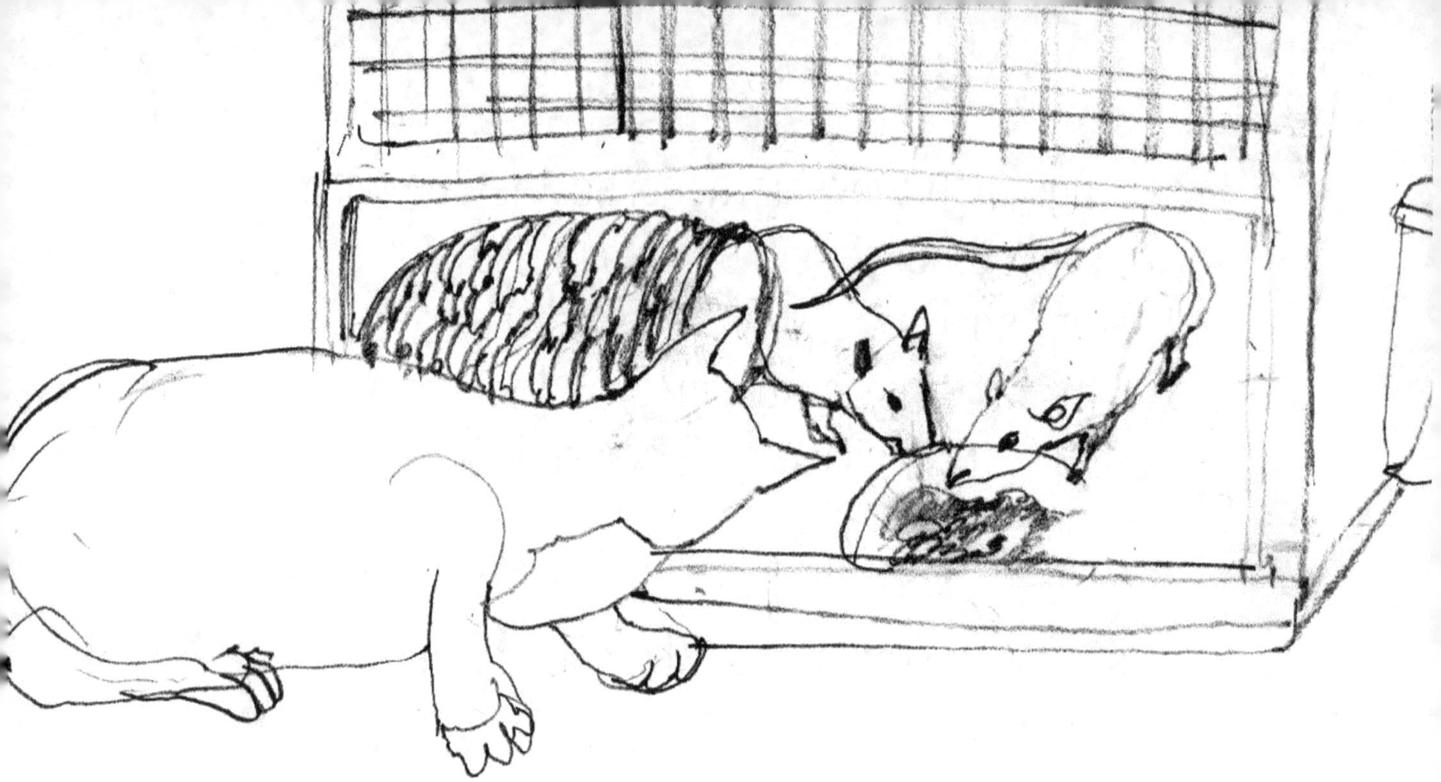

Ship's cats were respected mousers. Protectors of the Egyptian grains, they sailed on Phoenician, Roman and Viking trade routes throughout Europe.

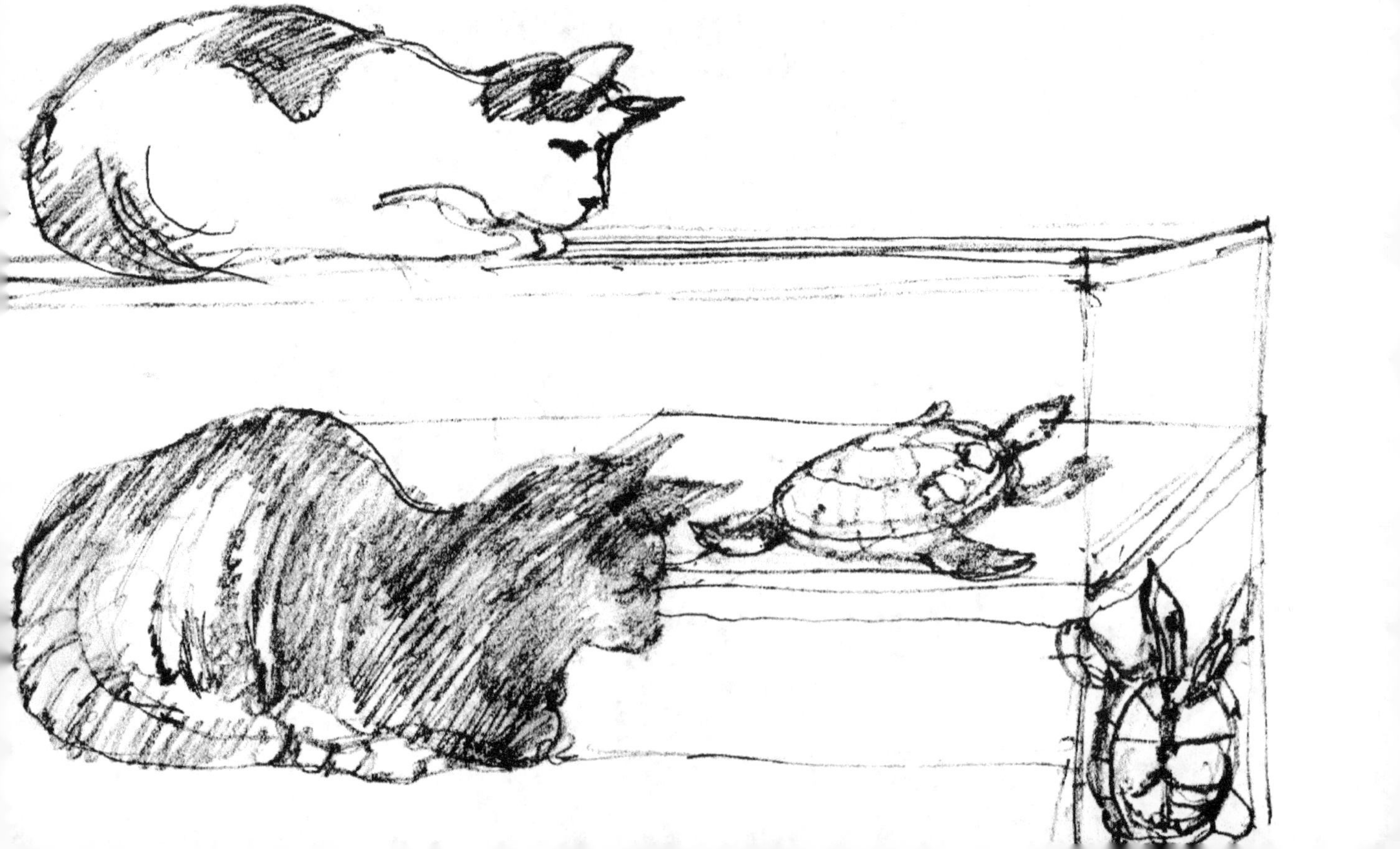

Christopher Columbus discovery of the
present day Bahamas came with domesticated
cats that spawned the American short hair
breed. One of the explored islands was named
Cat Island.

Unlike humans, who would be poisoned by
drinking seawater, a cat's kidney filters the
salt. Cats can drink seawater.

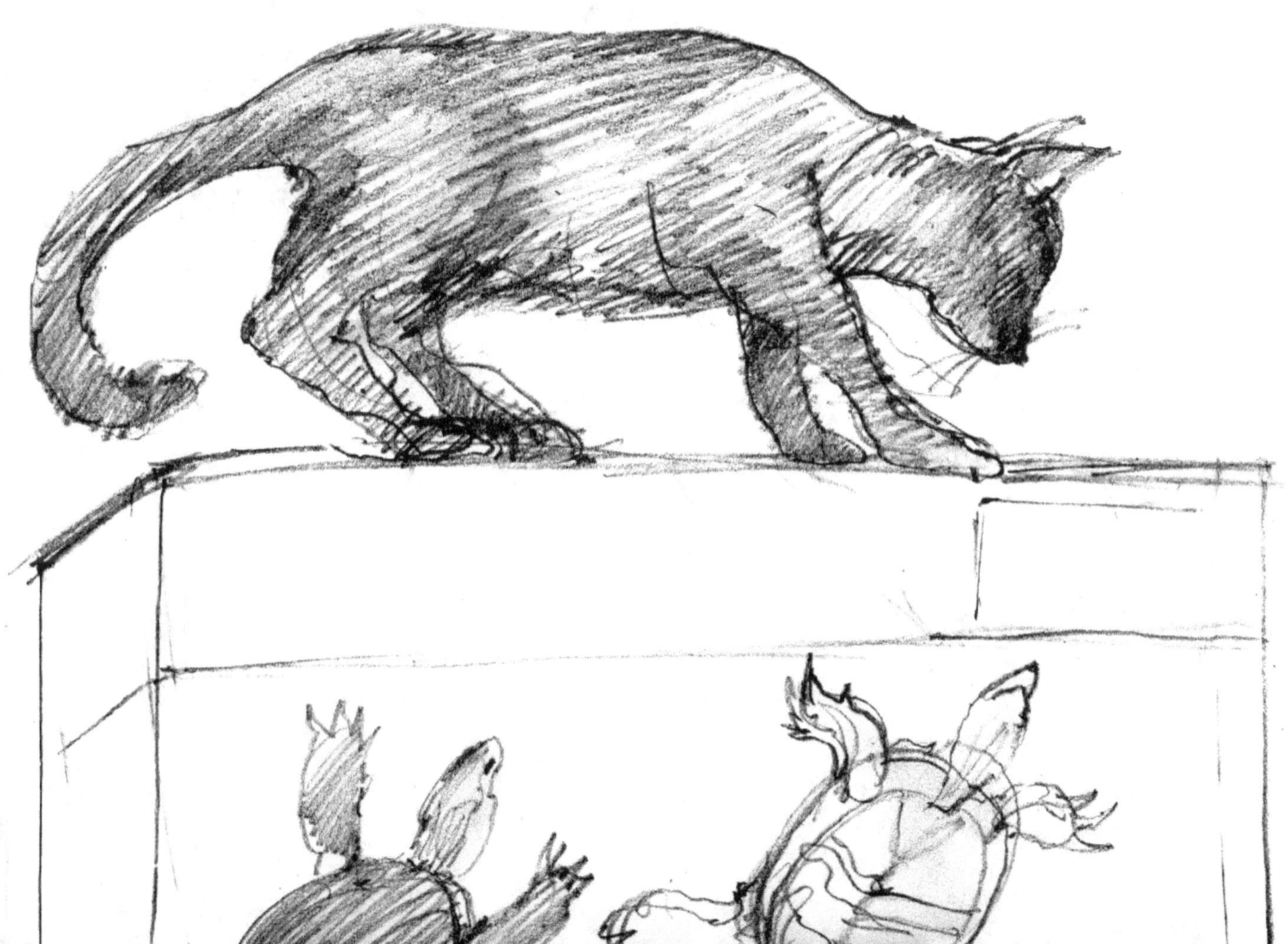

An ancient Hebrew legend tells of Noah praying to God to deliver him from the rats who were eating the grain on the Ark. God's answer to Noah was a lion's sneeze that produced the hairball that is a cat.

Mohammad's favorite cat was a Tabby breed he named Muezza. The word tabby comes from the word Attabiyh, a neighborhood in Bagdad, Iraq. Attabiyh is where curvy striped patterns on silk were created.

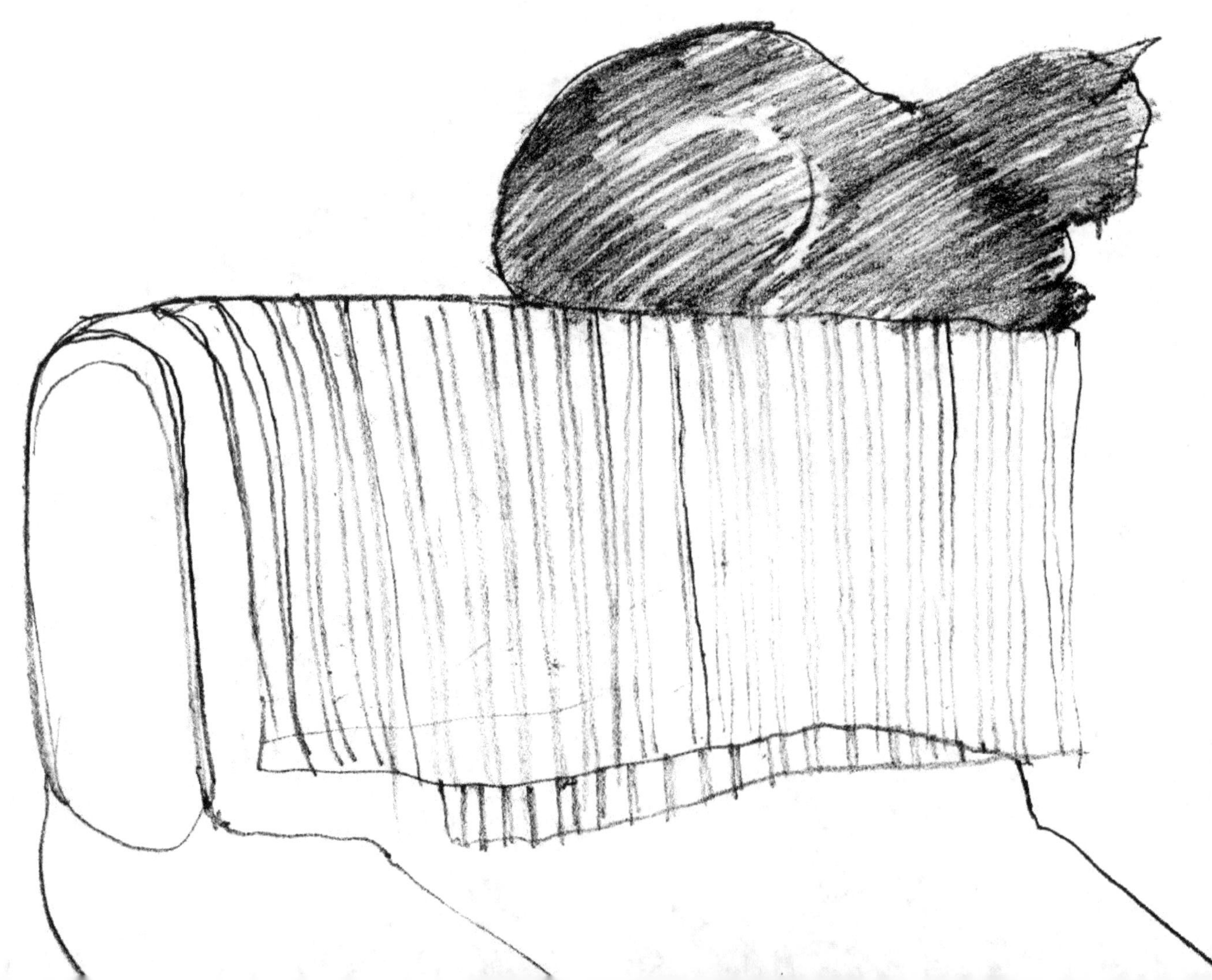

In Japan, Buddhists ordained
that the body of a cat is a
momentary resting place for
the souls of the most
enlightened spiritual believers.

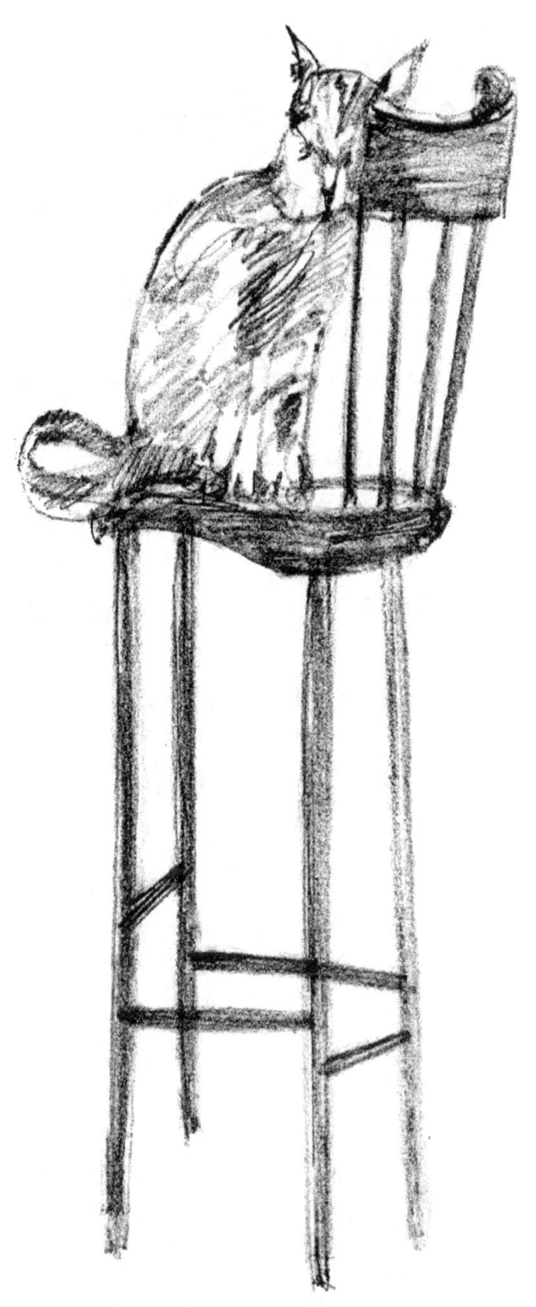

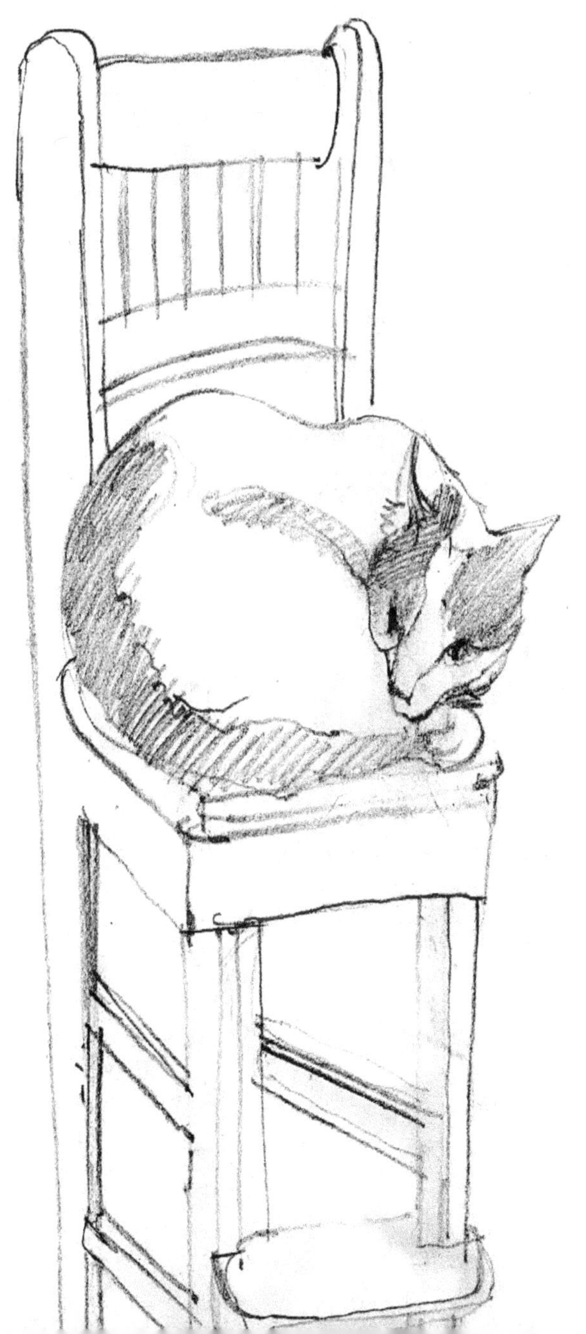

It has been found that a
cat purrs at a particular
frequency that leads to
the healing of sore bones
and muscles.

Cats were mentioned in medieval heresy trials. In 1309 the Dominican inquisitor Etienne de Bourbon affirmed the secret heretical rites of the Templars kissing the butt of black cats. The theologian Arnold of Liege spoke of a popular proverb about a cat playing with a mouse was how the devil played with human souls. In the Spanish inquisition they would throw these cats from church towers on holy days. Enhancing an explosion of the rat population and the "Black Death" plague.

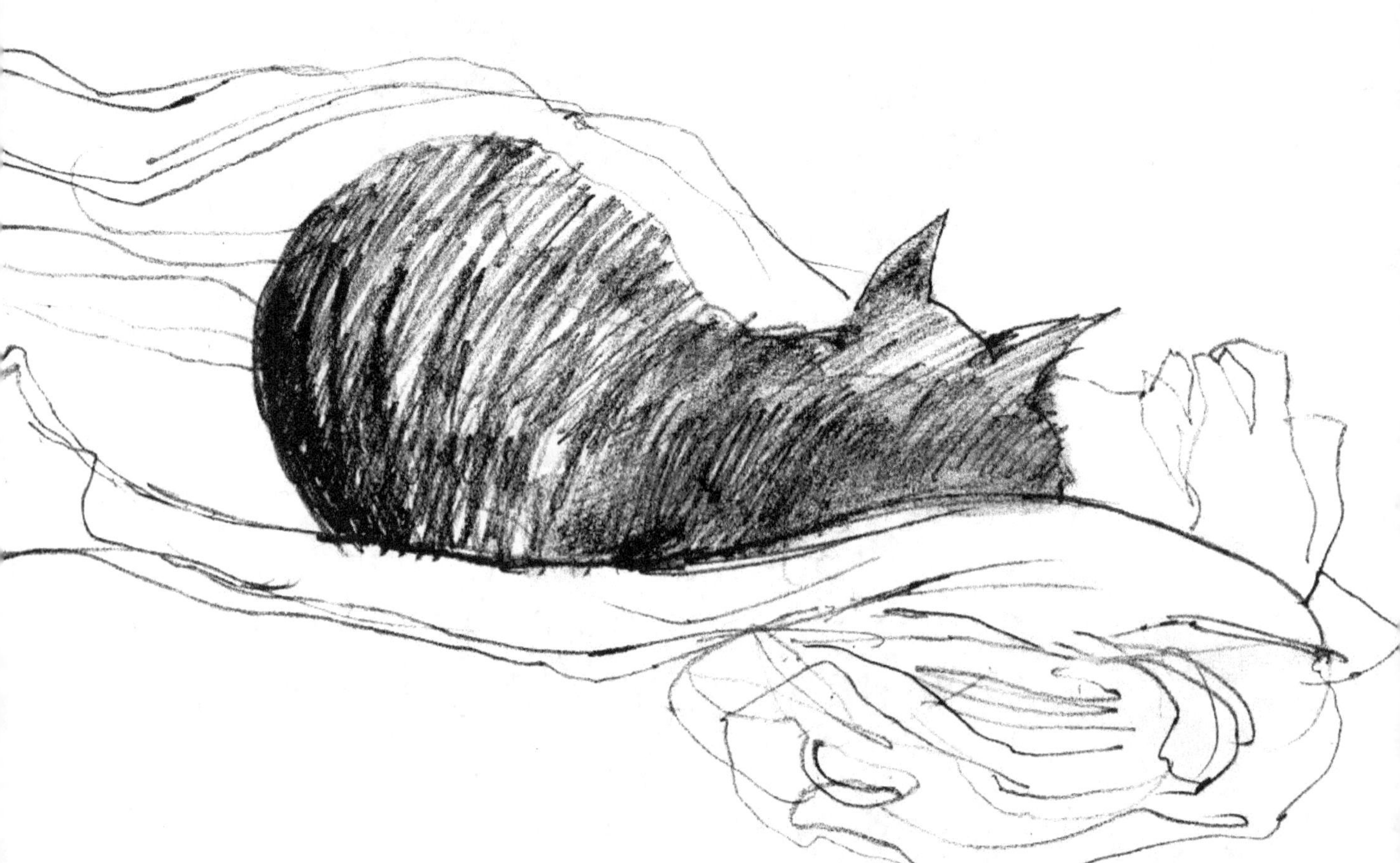

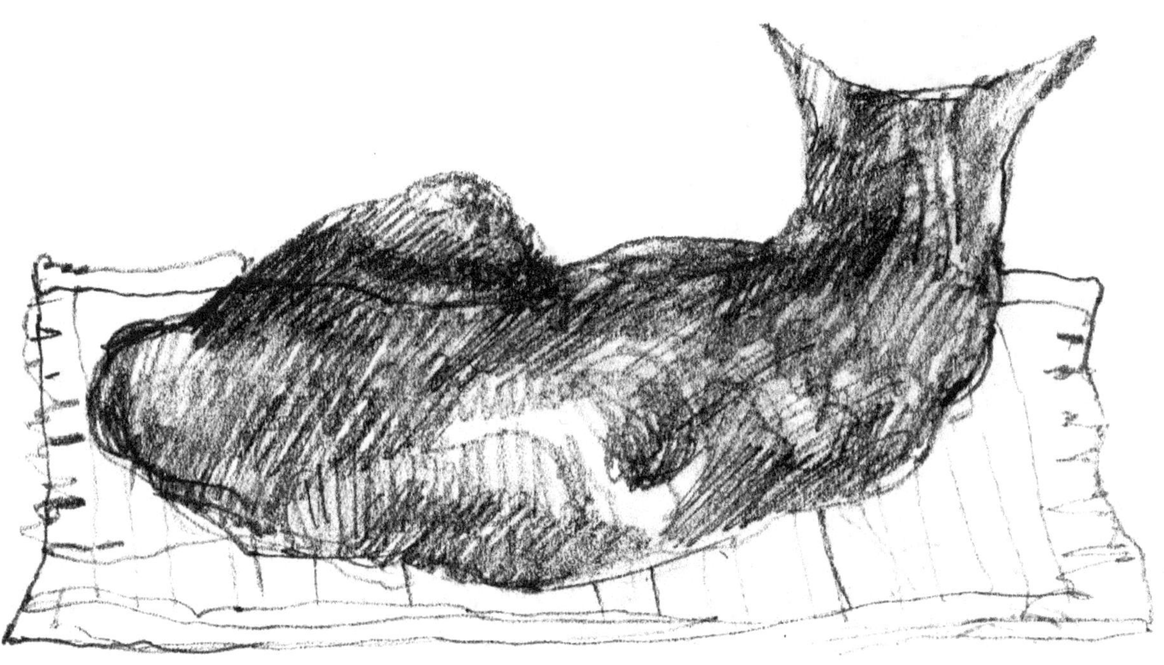

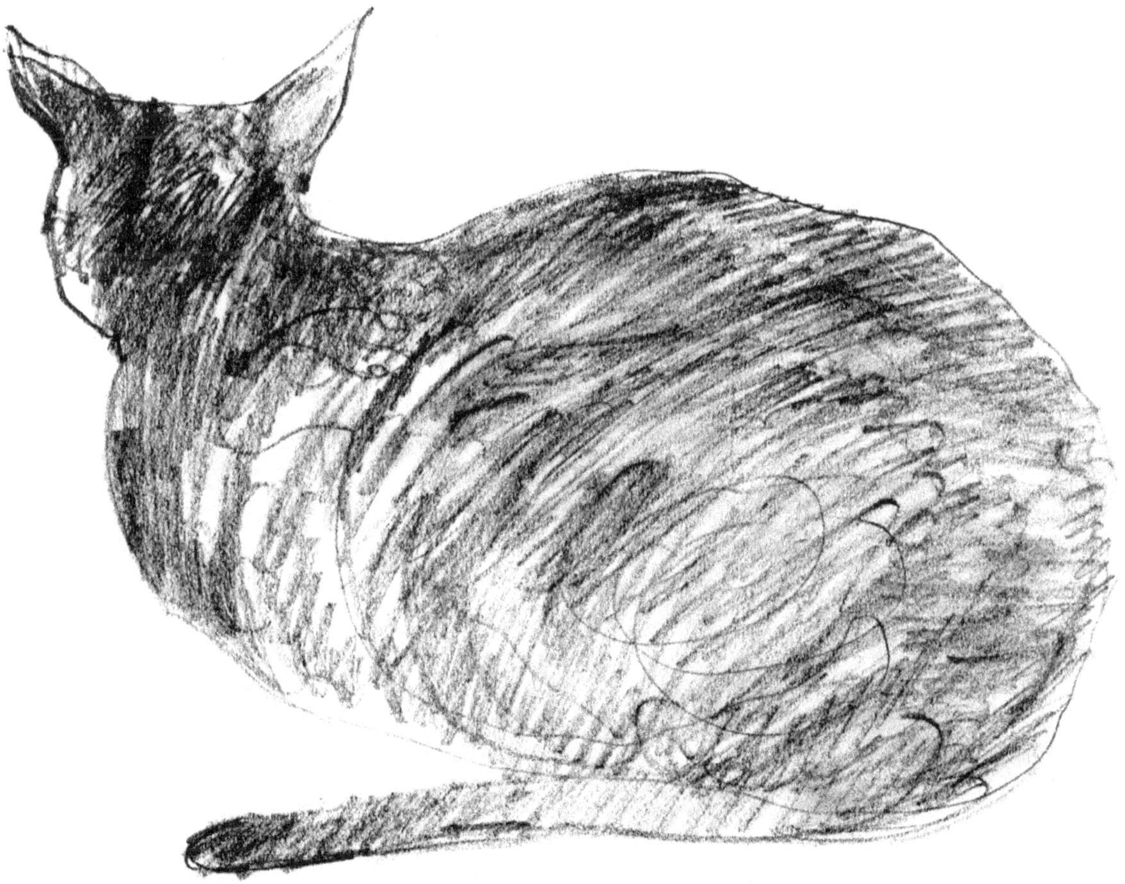

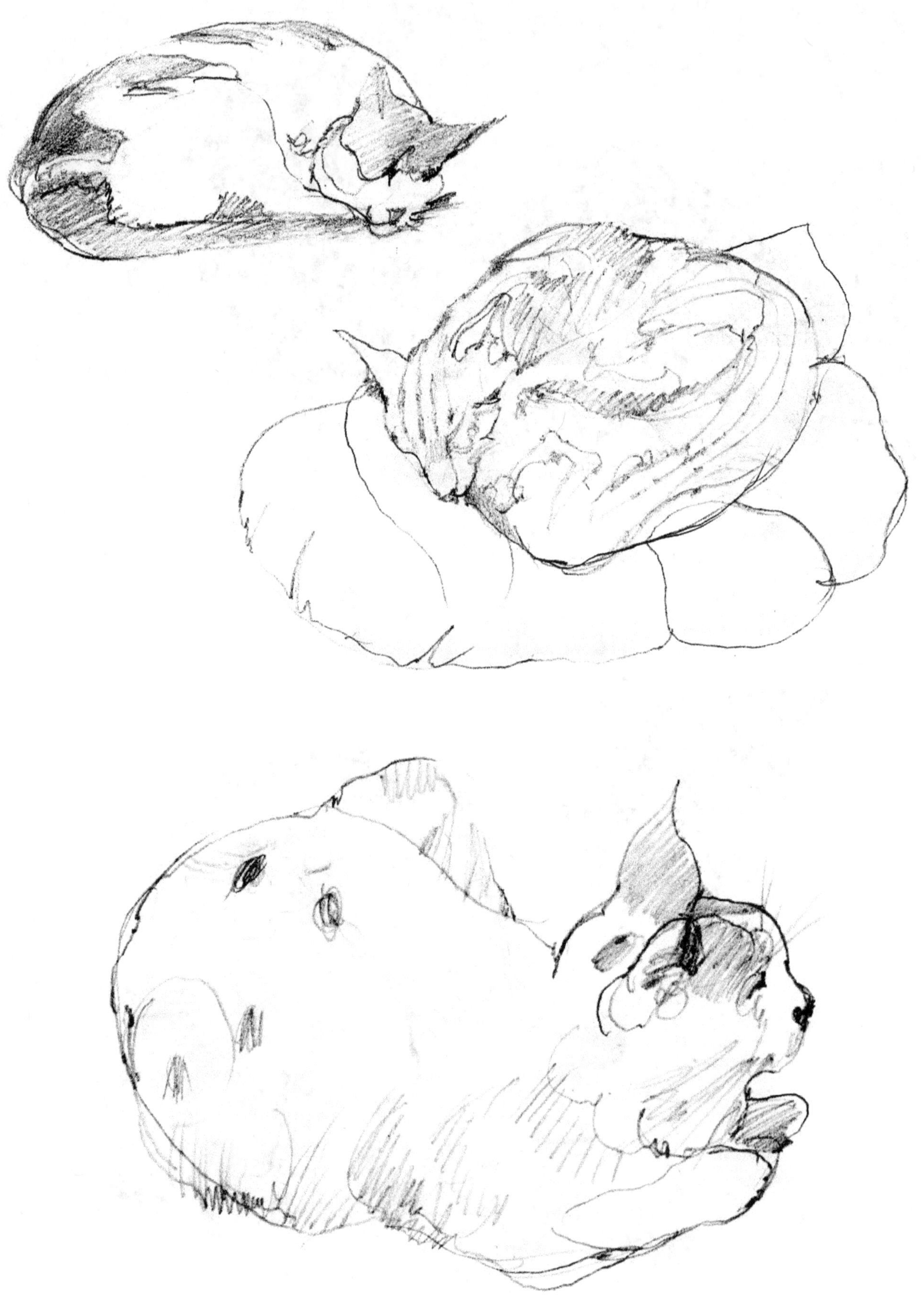

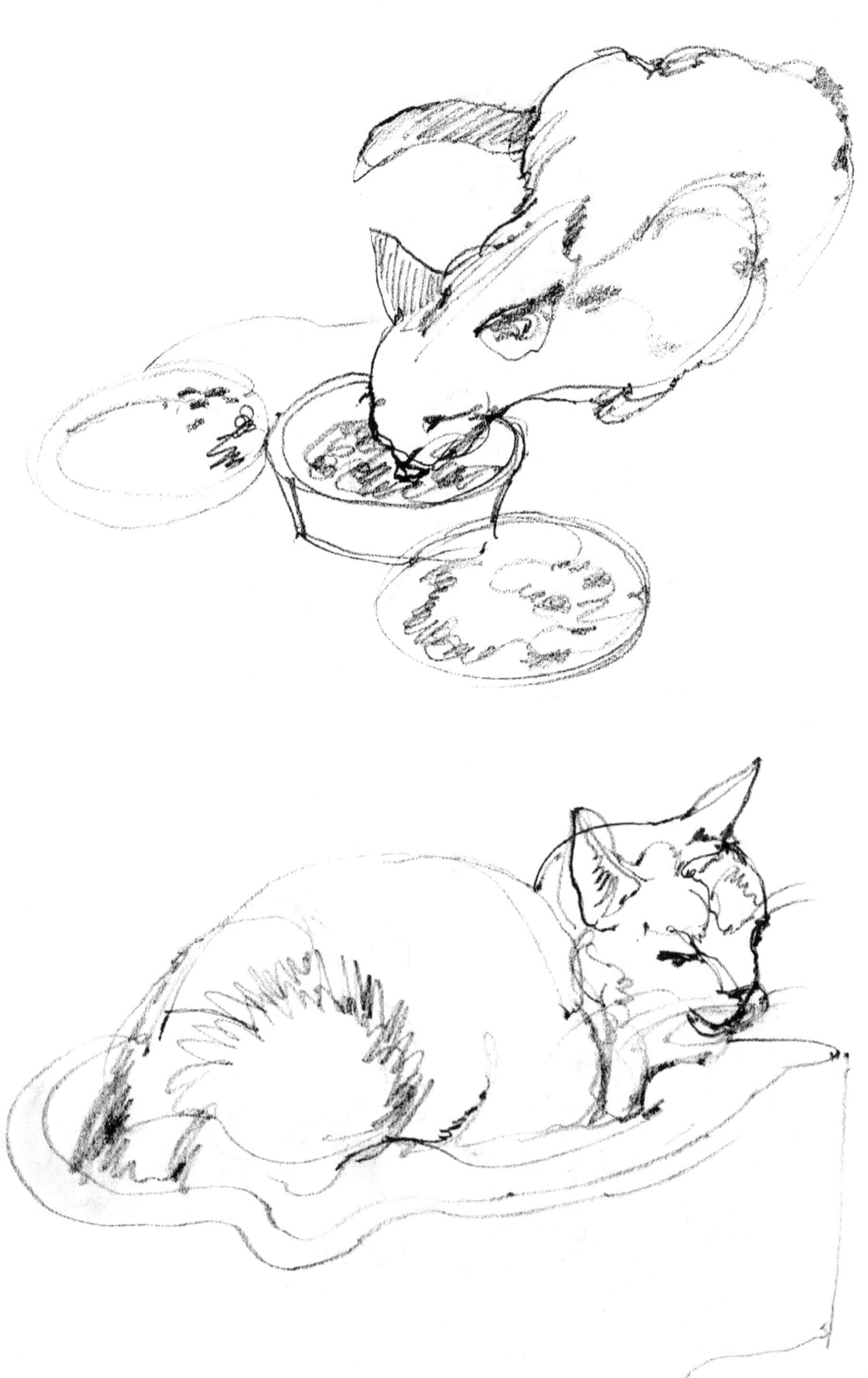

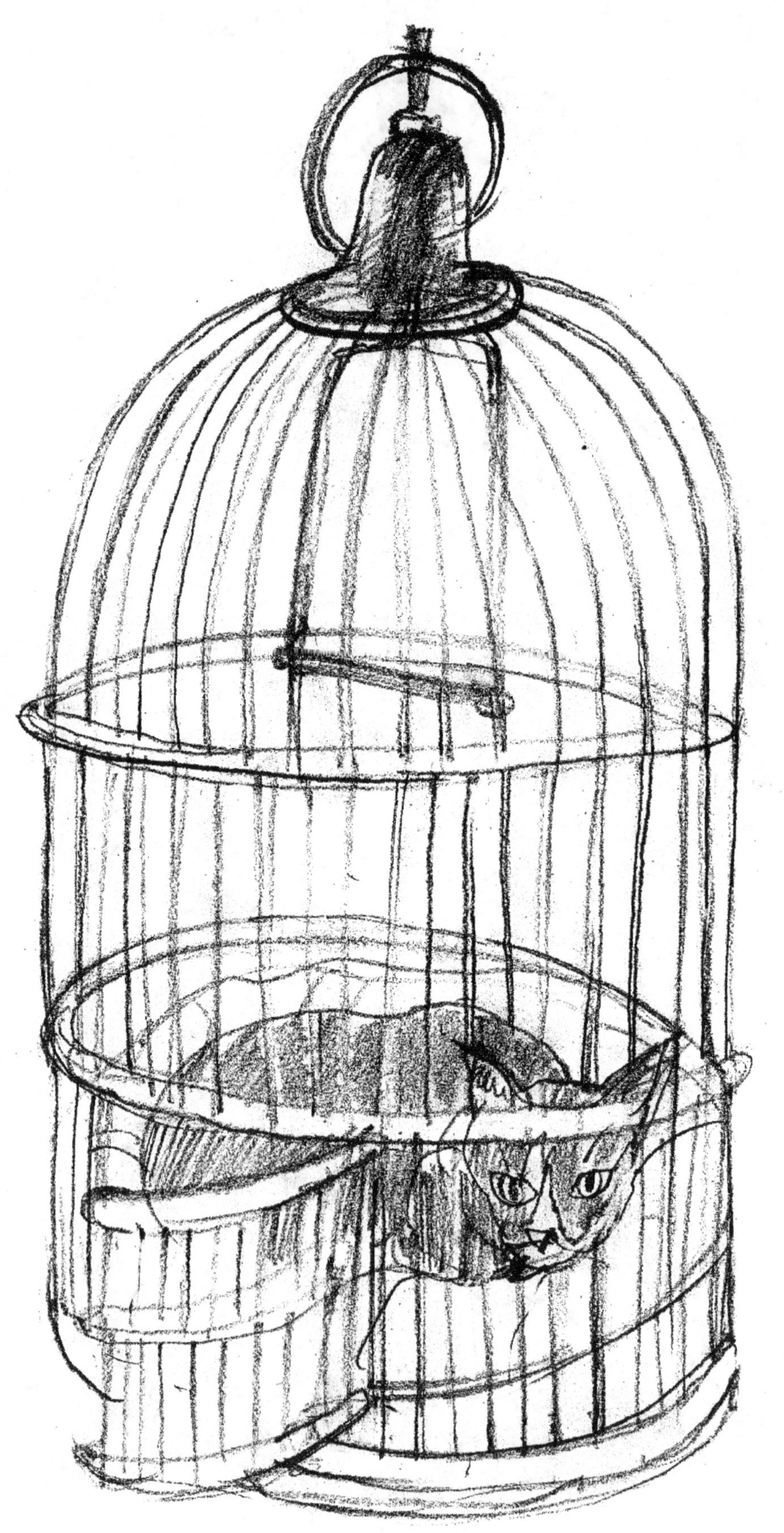

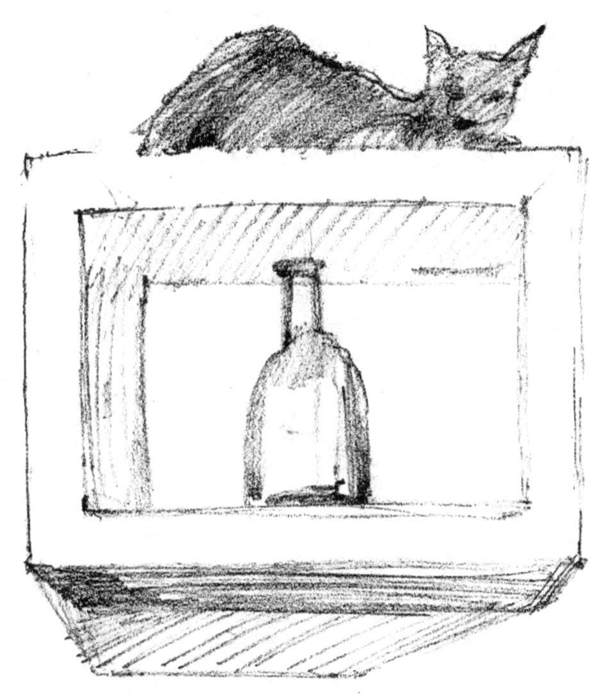

"Sitting in the cat bird seat" means being perched in an optimum position in life, or hunting prey, sitting pretty, ready to bounce.

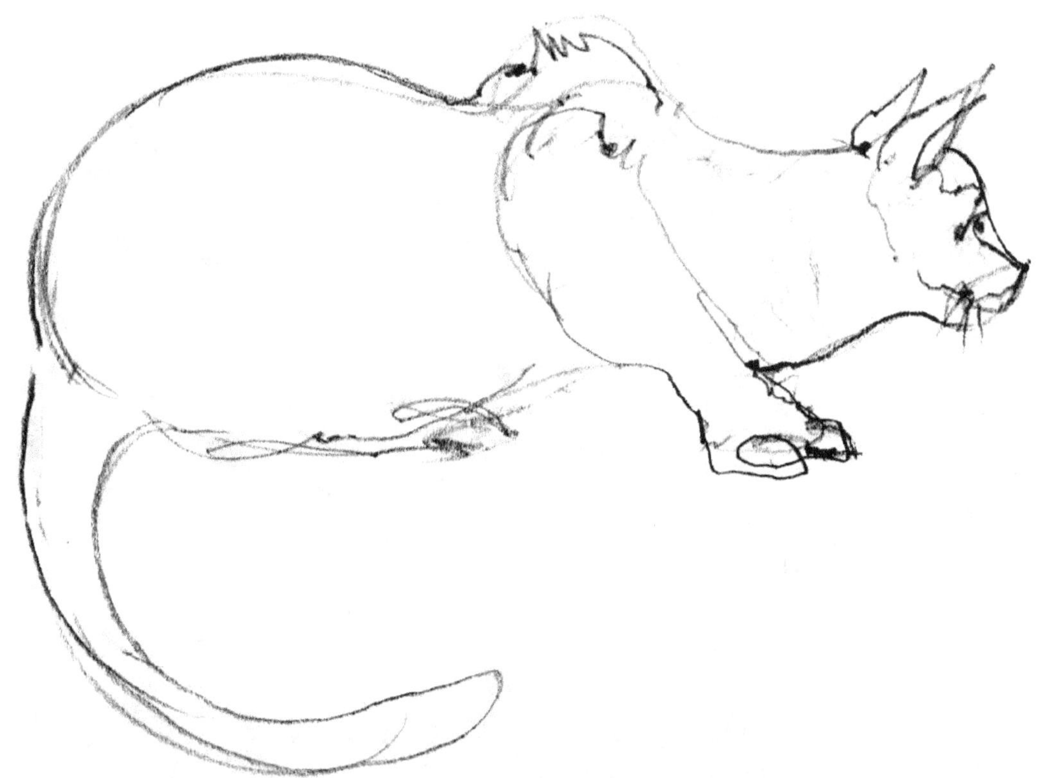

The Abyssinian breed of cat was found to have 90 percent human DNA. In comparison, the chimpanzee carries 98 percent human DNA.
The banana has 60 percent.

A house cat shares 95.6 percent of the genetic makeup of wild cats.

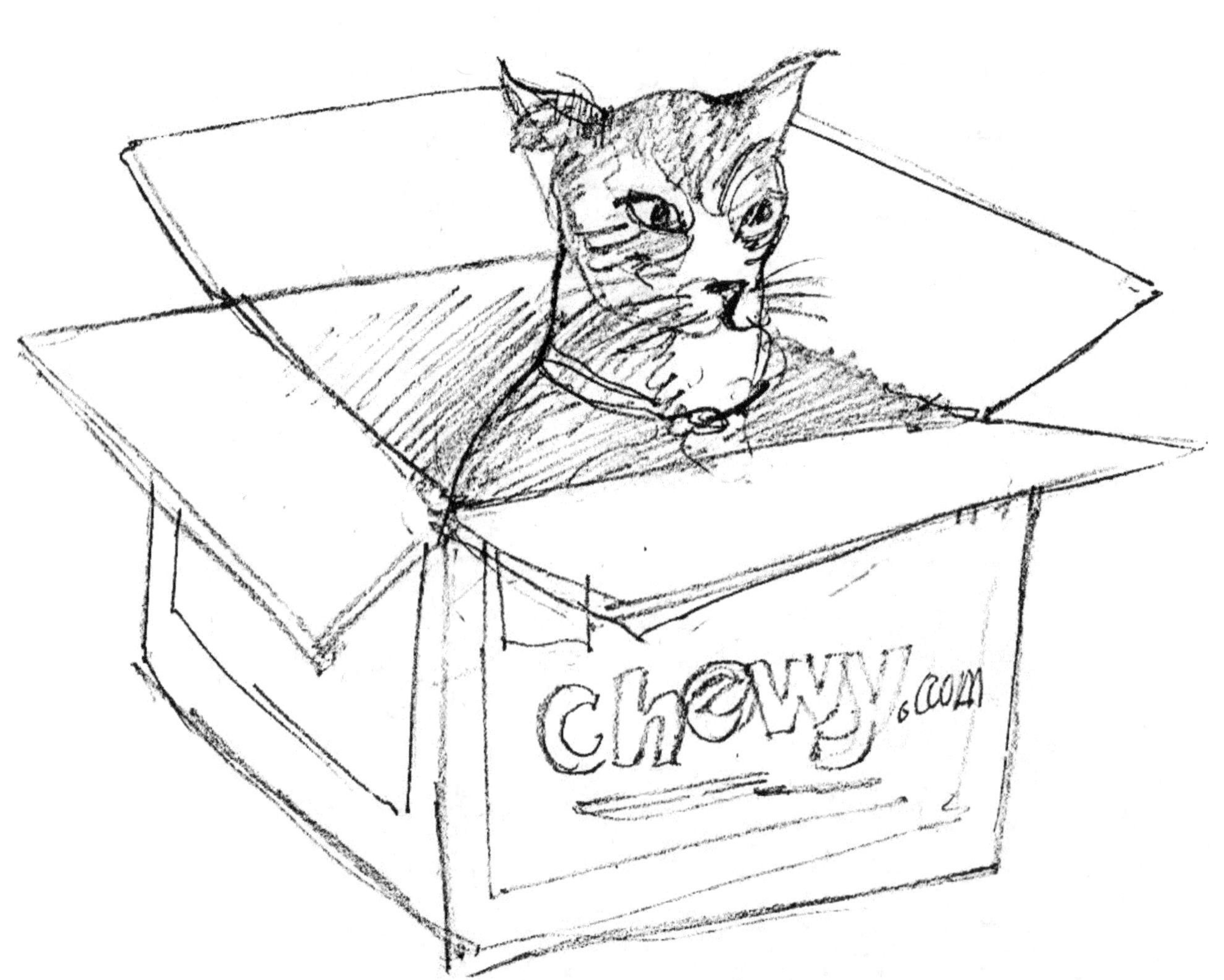

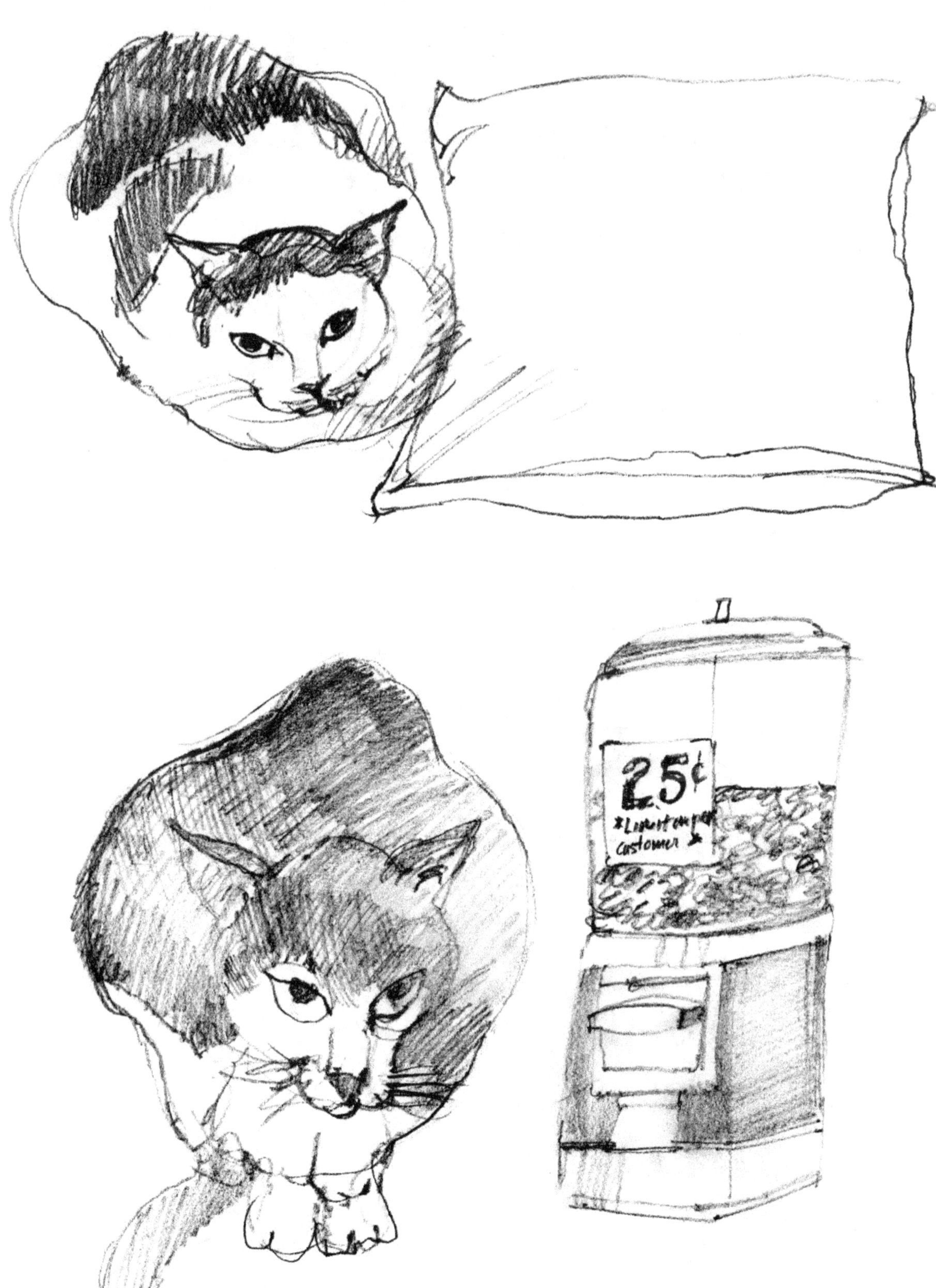

25¢
*Limit one per
customer*

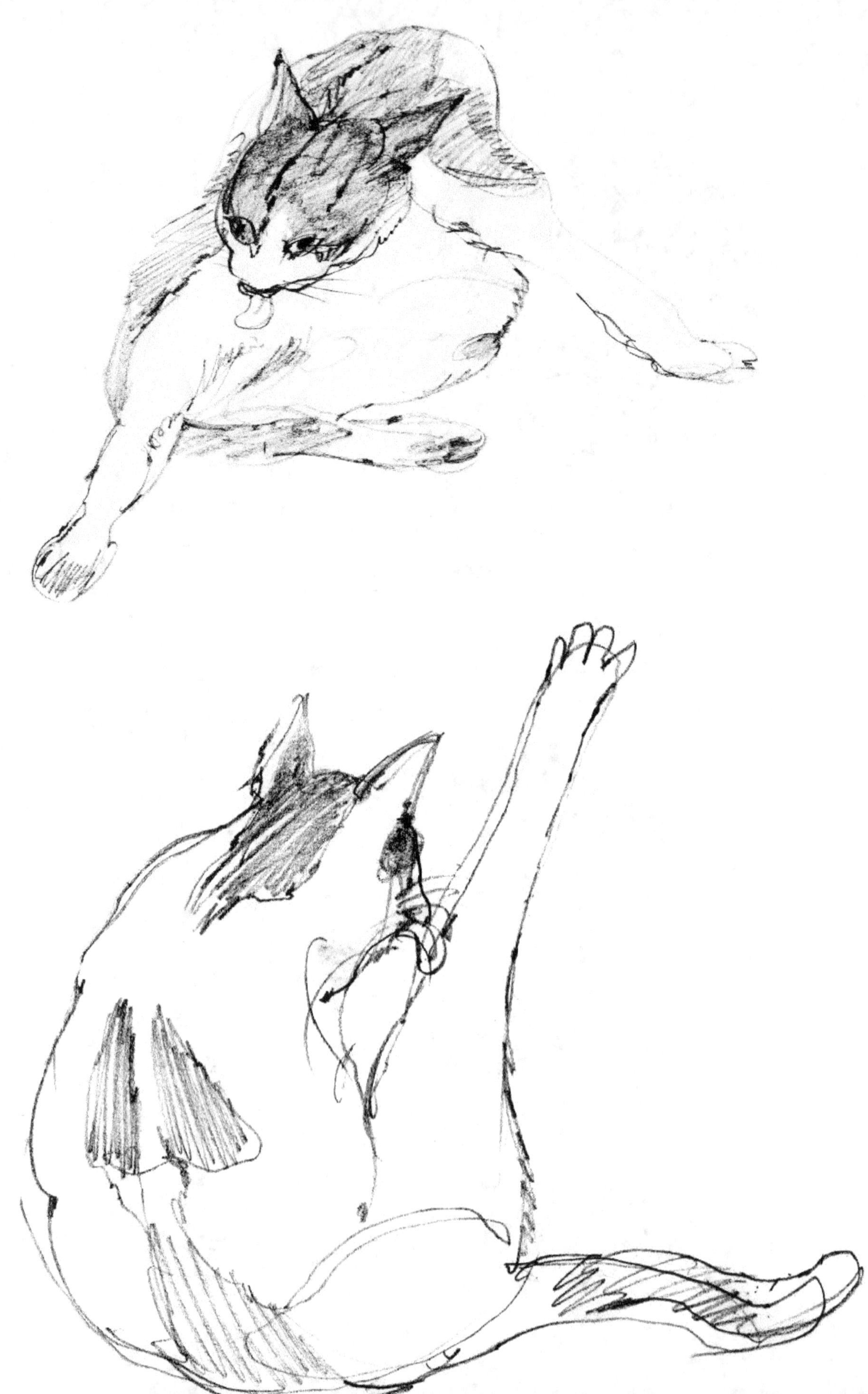

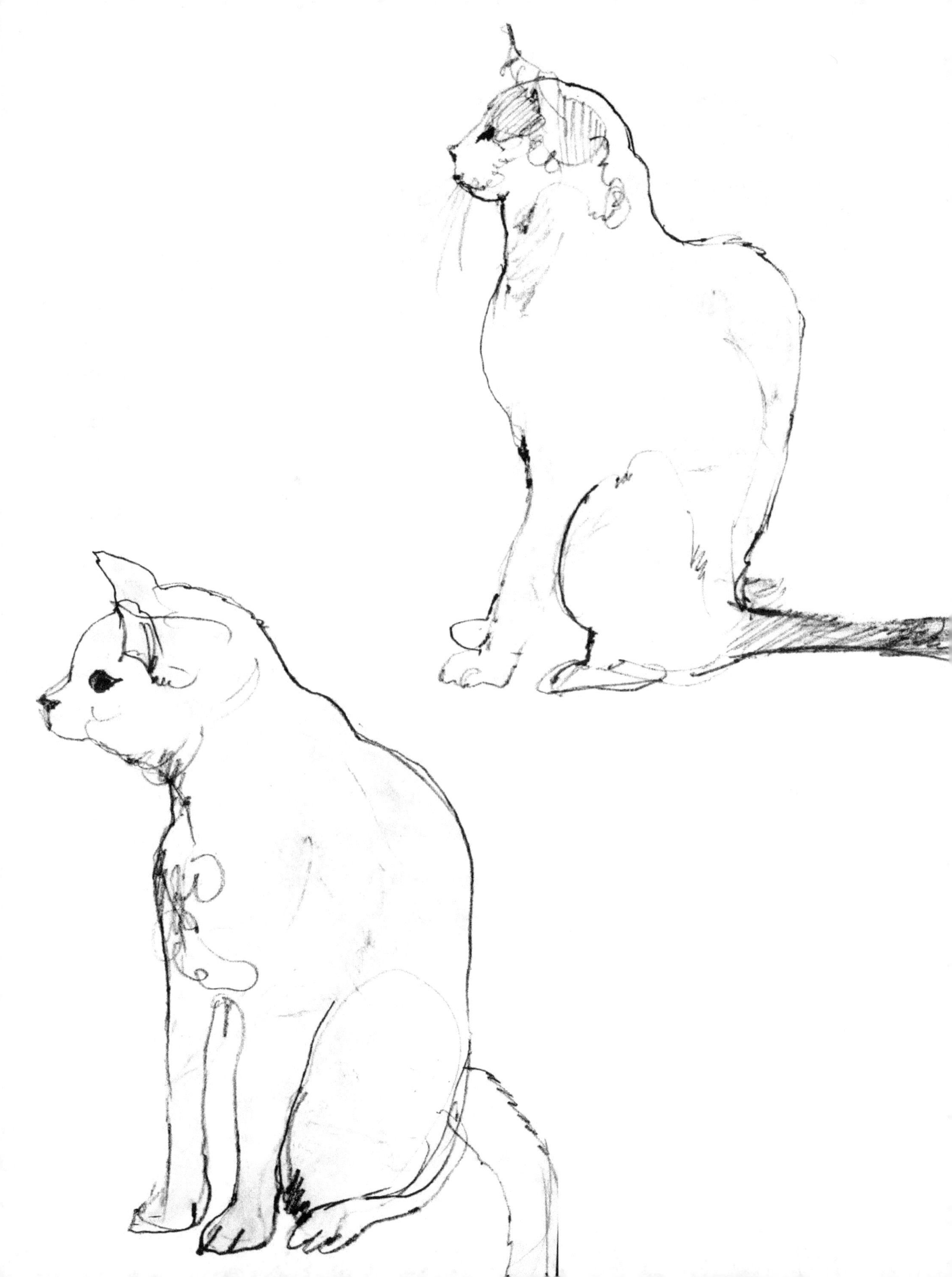

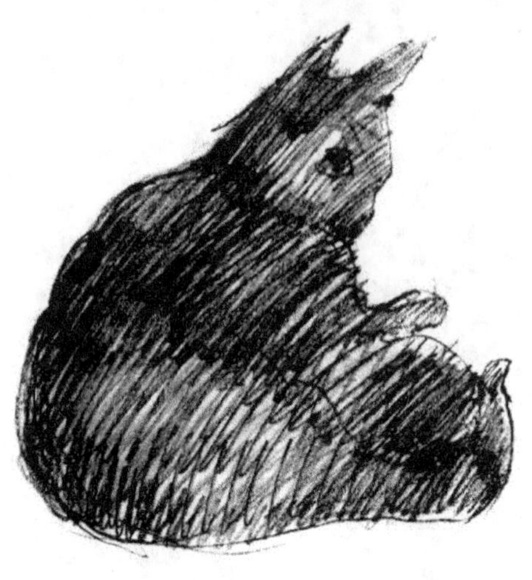

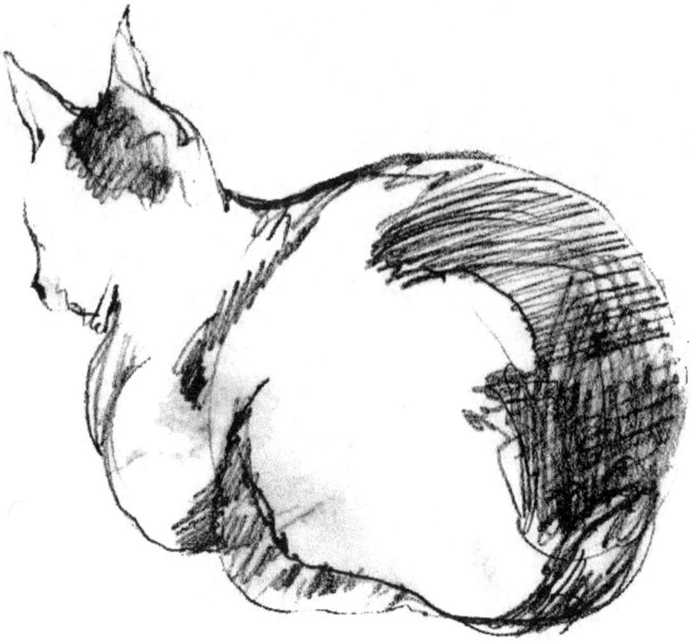

Purring, trilling, hissing,
growling, squawking,
chirping, clicking, and
grunting are among the
hundred cat sounds spoken
among themselves.
Meowing has evolved as
cat speech for humans
alone.

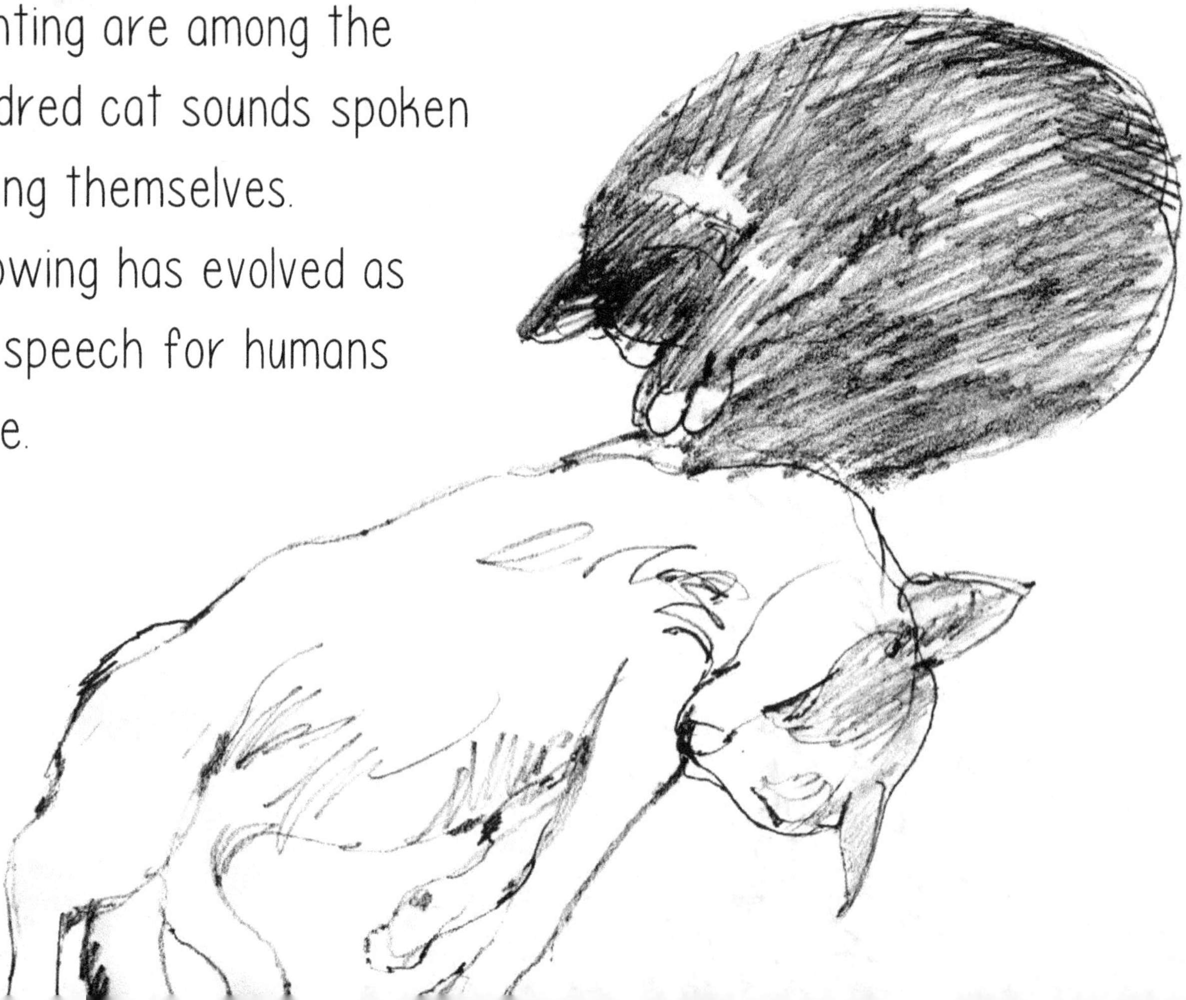

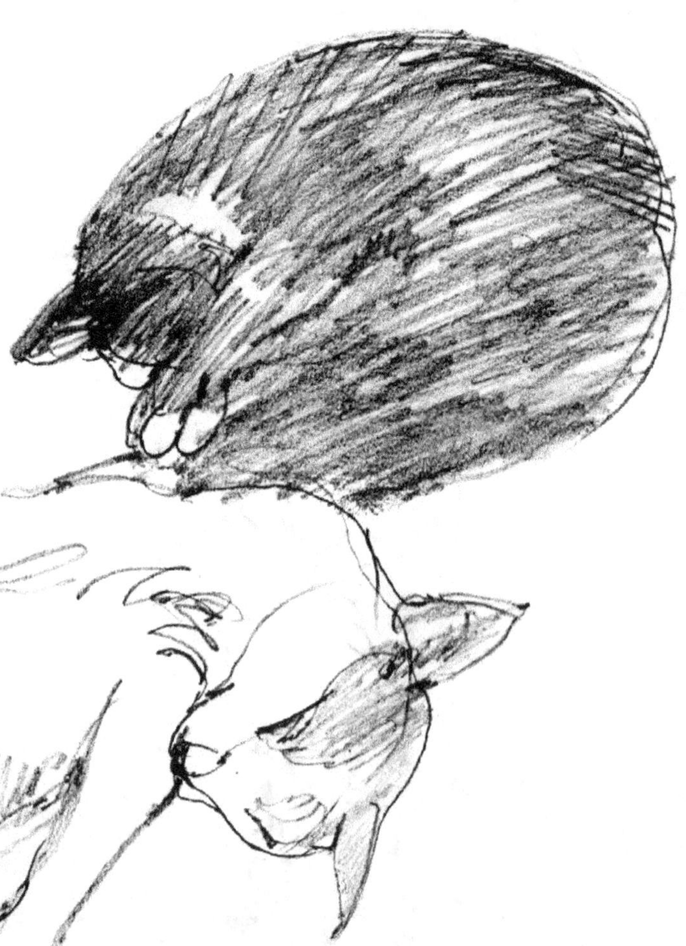

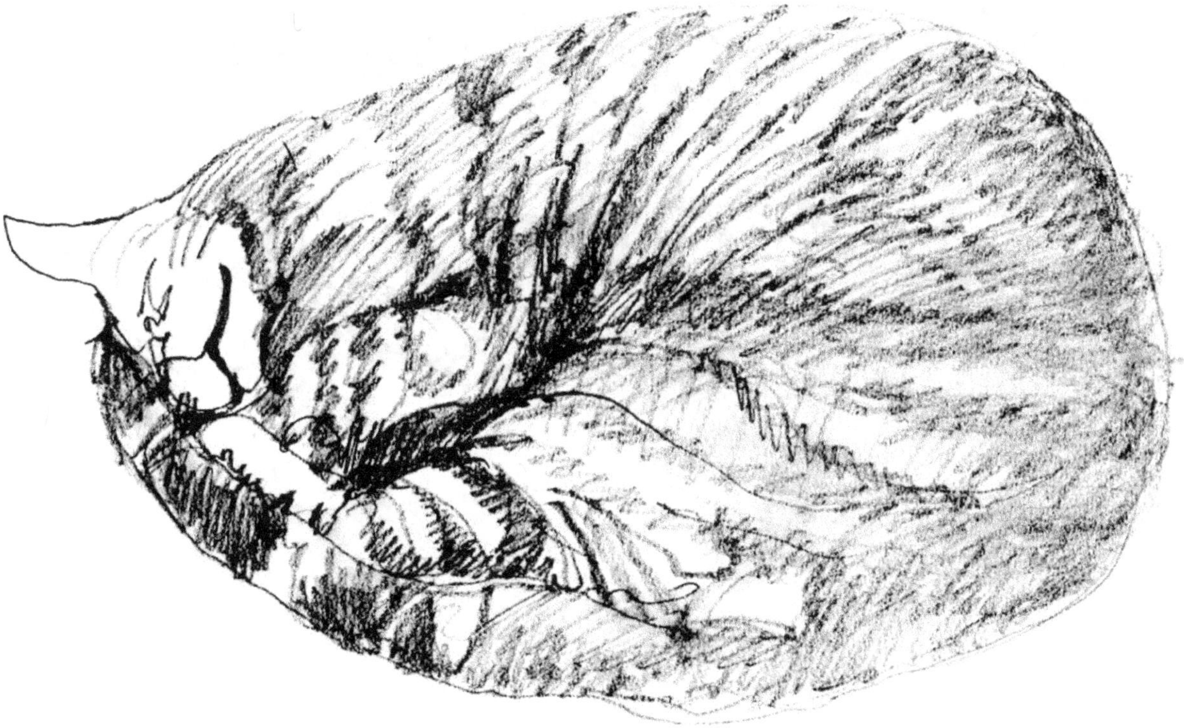

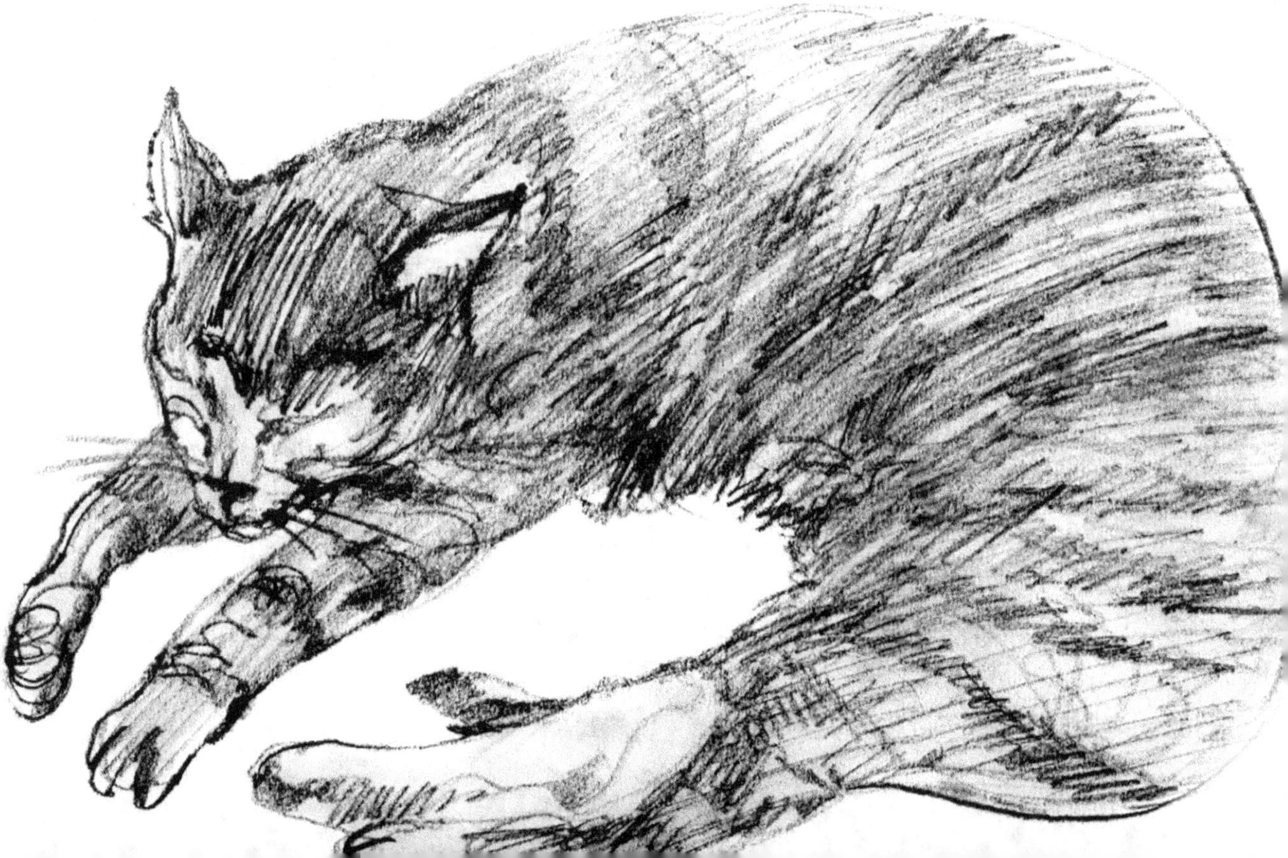

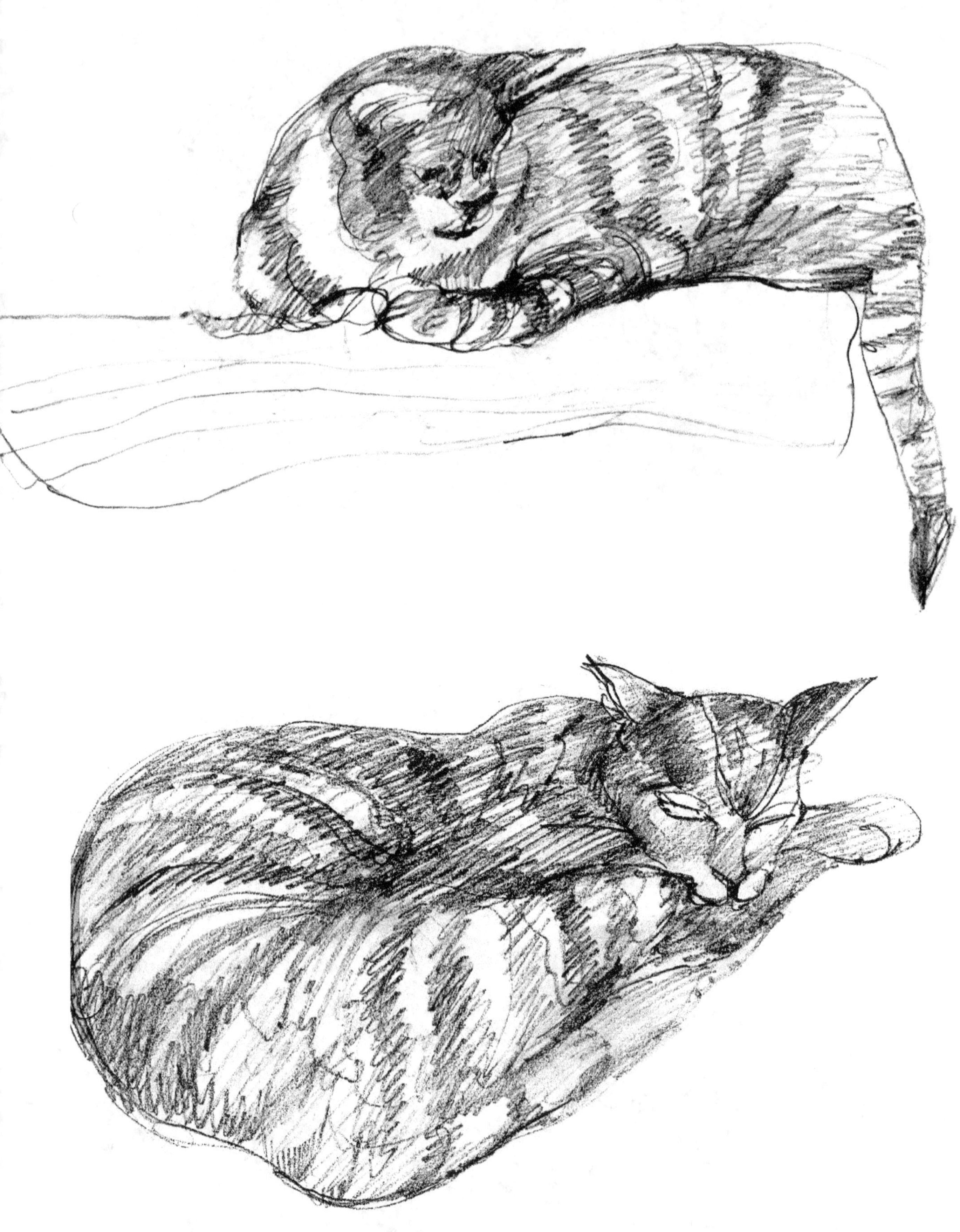

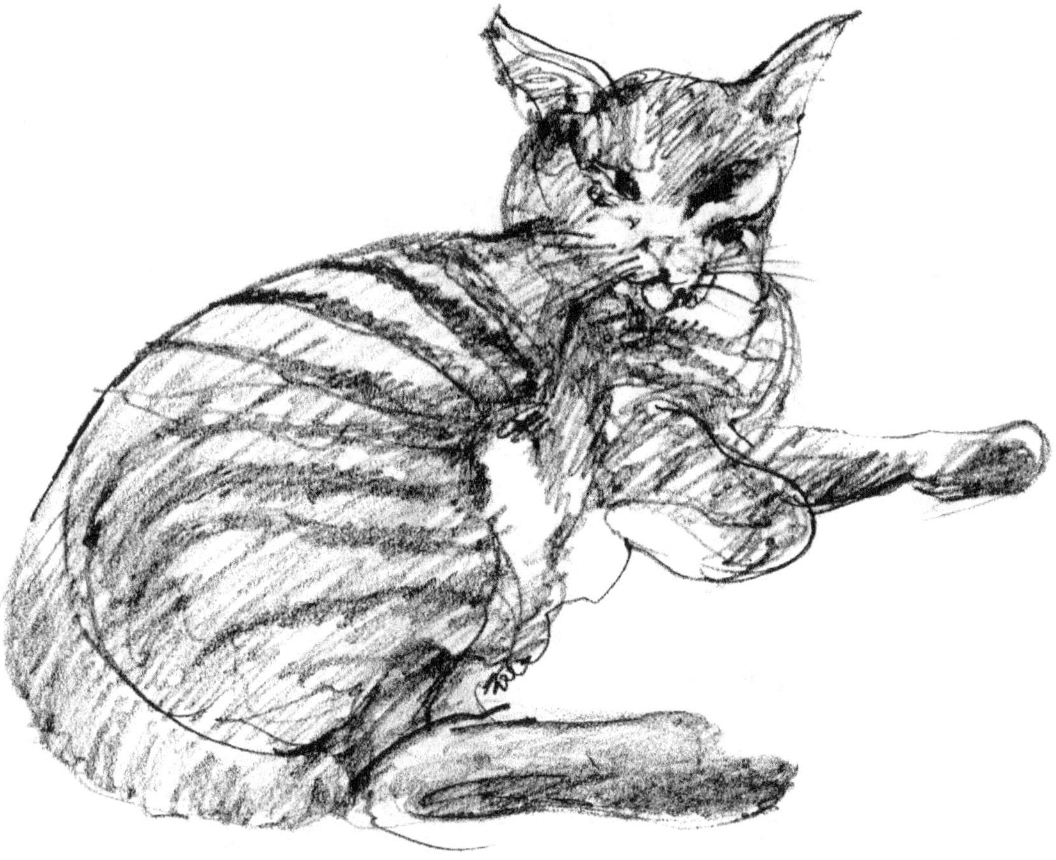

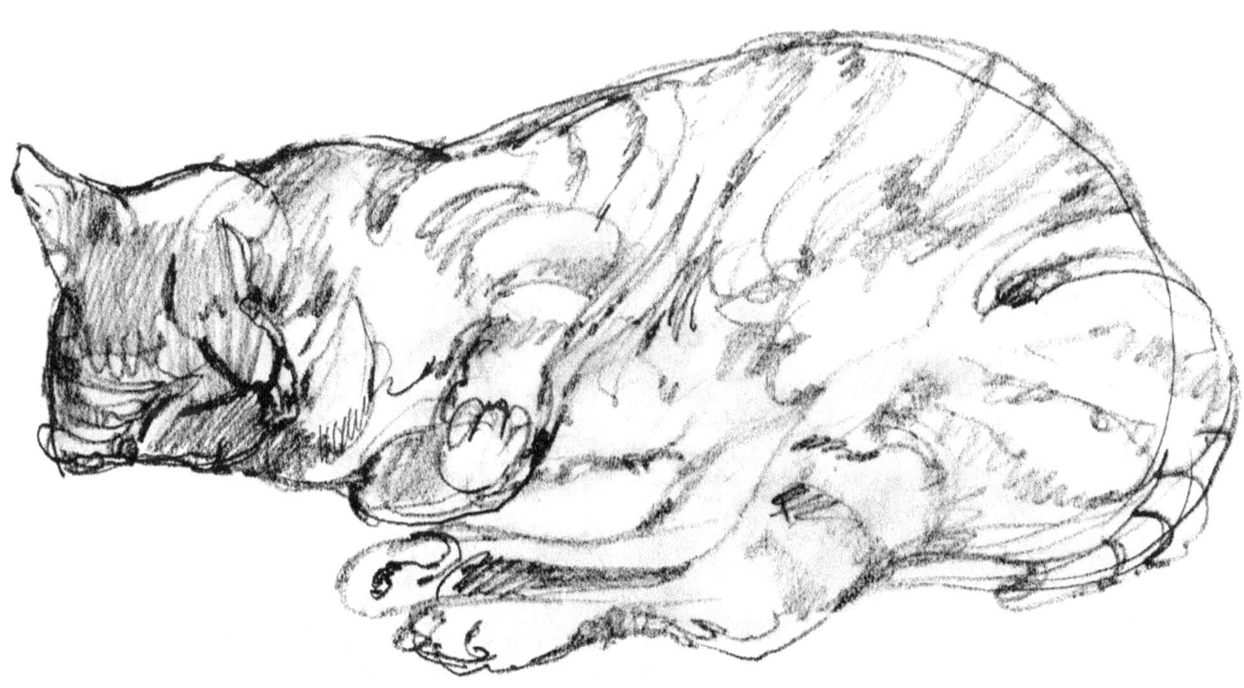

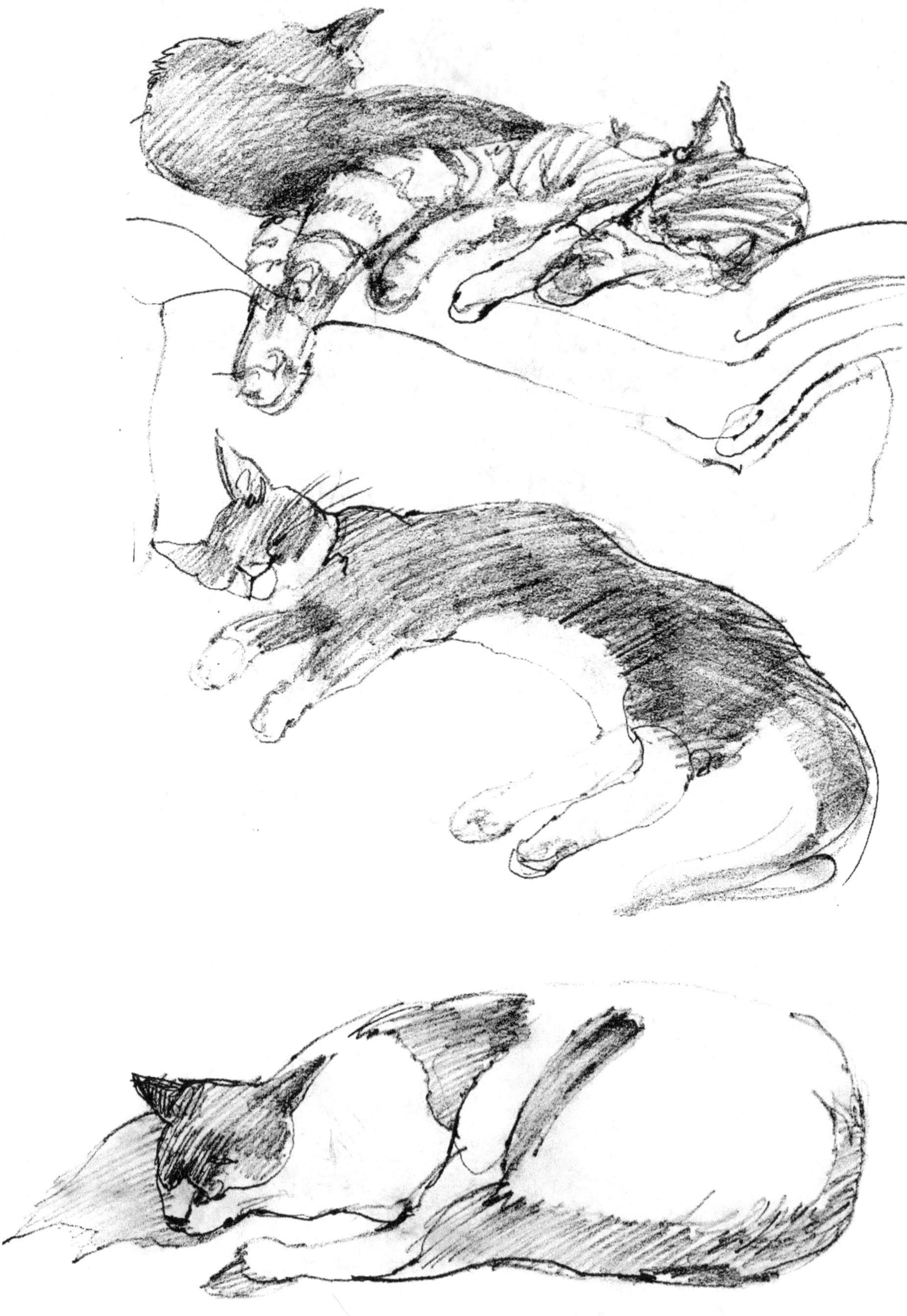

Cats spend up to 70 percent of their day sleeping and 15 percent of that waking day is devoted to grooming.

A cat's brain is biologically more similar to a human then a dog. Both have a similar brain part dedicated to emotions.

A cat heart beats twice as fast as the human heart. And a cat can dream with rapid eye movement.

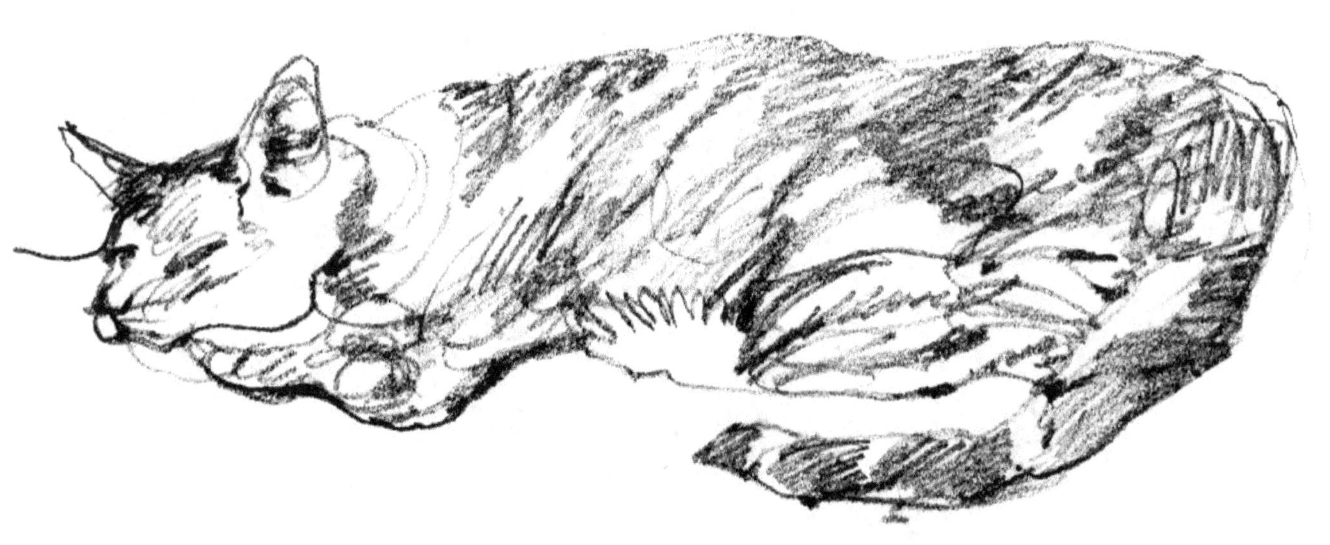

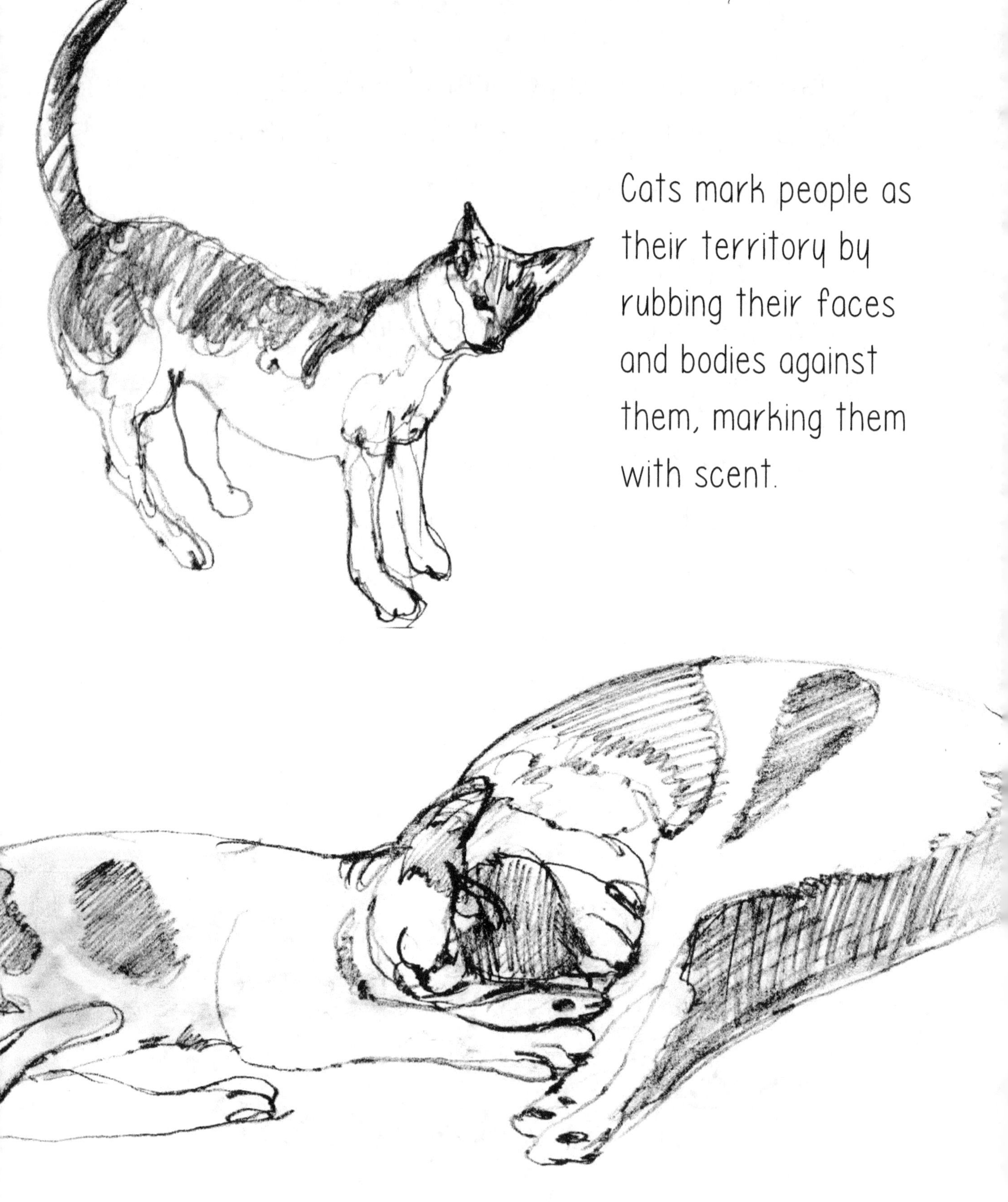

Cats mark people as
their territory by
rubbing their faces
and bodies against
them, marking them
with scent.

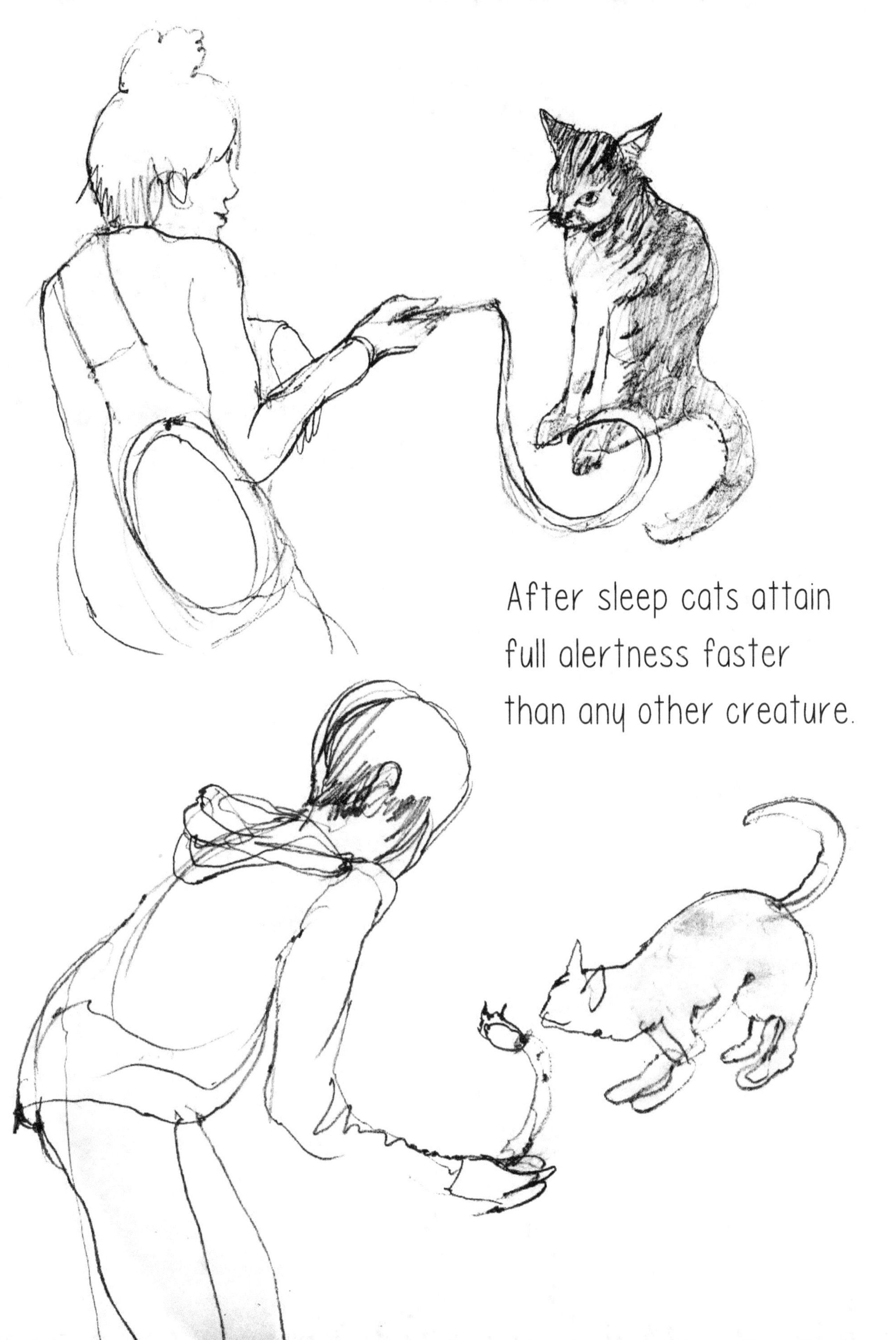

After sleep cats attain
full alertness faster
than any other creature.

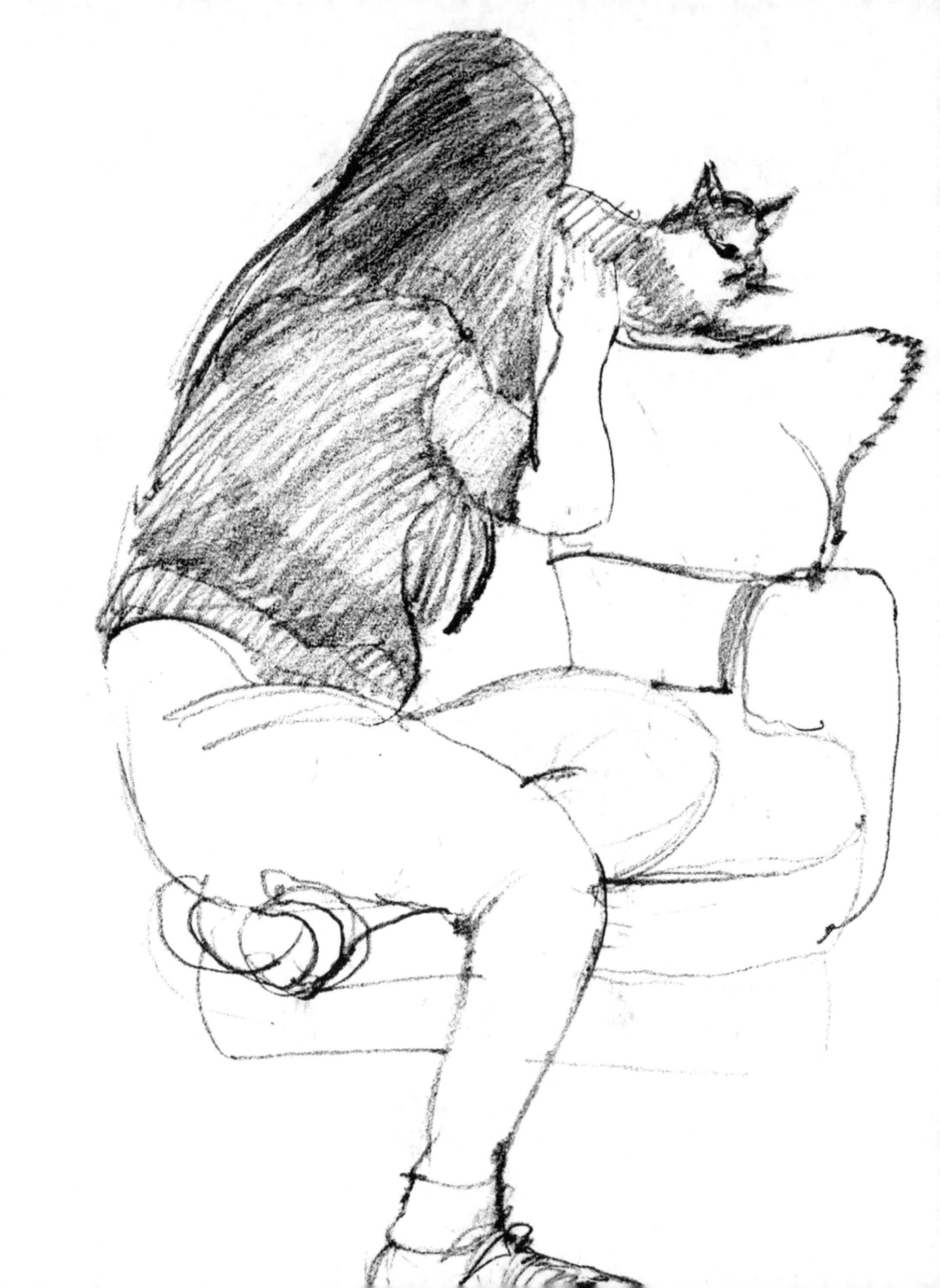

Mary Todd Lincoln once was asked if her husband, Abraham, had any hobbies. Her response was "cats." Isaac Newton's cat named "Spithead", distracted his experiments by scratching at the door. His response was the invention of the first cat door flap that remains at Cambridge University, England, today.

Superstition suggests that cats have more than one life. In Turkey and Arabia, a cat's lives are six. In Germany and Brazil seven lives. Cat lore in other countries speak of nine.

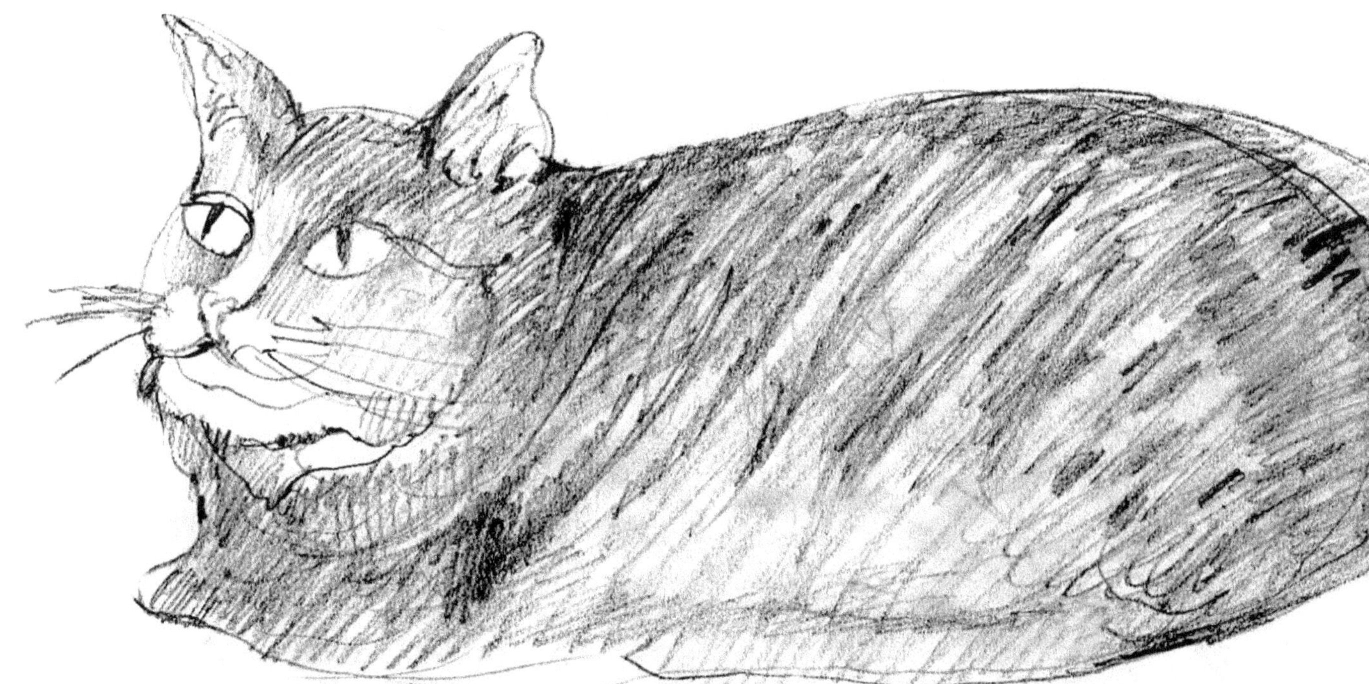

Francois Rene de Chateaubriand, French Nobleman and writer wrote: "I love the cat, that independent and almost ungrateful temper which prevents it from attaching itself to anyone. The cat lives alone, has no need for society, does not obey except when it likes, and pretends to sleep that it may see the world more clearly, and scratches everything that it can scratch. Buffon has belied the cat. I am laboring at its rehabilitation, and hope to make it a tolerably good sort of animal, as times go"

"The smallest feline is a masterpiece."
Leonardo de Vince.

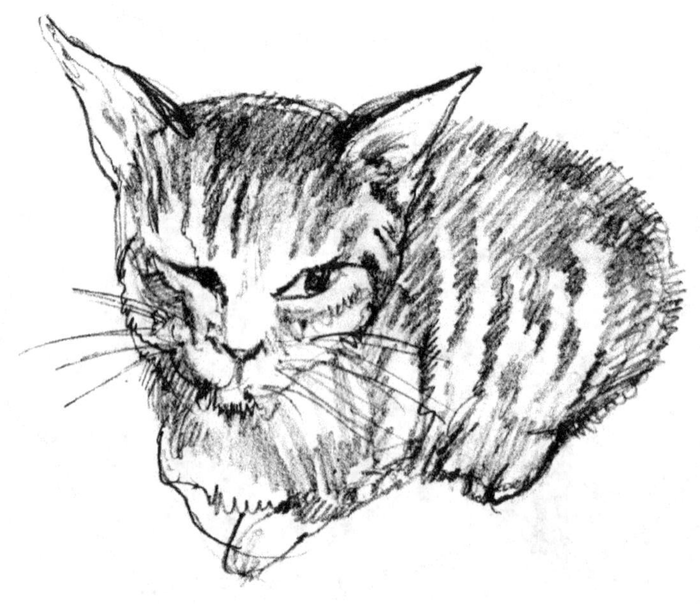

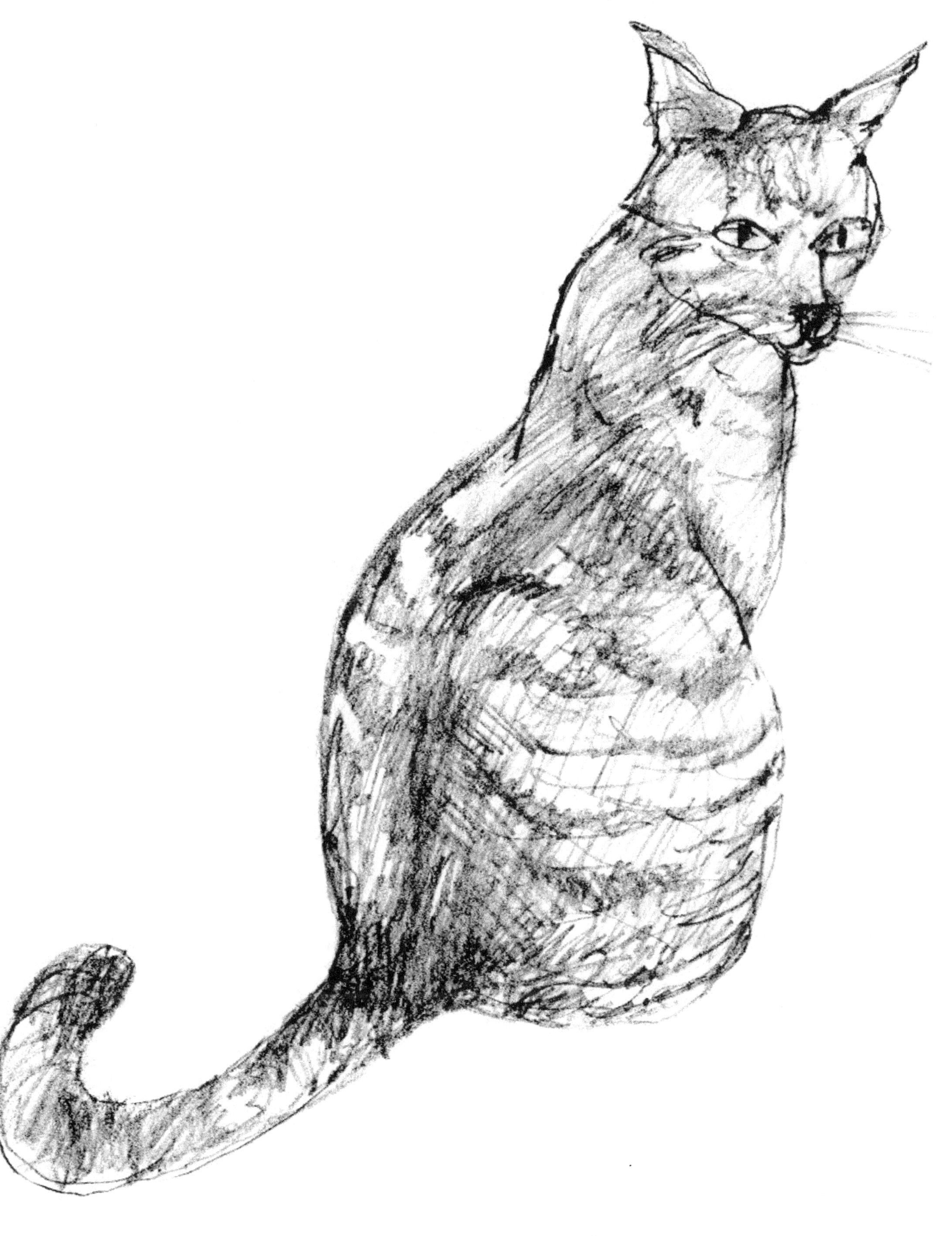

I dedicate this book to the cat lady's, Anne Levine, Annie Sullivan, and the volunteers at the Brooklyn Cat Café for allowing me to sketch their cats.

And for rescuing and finding homes for abandoned street cats with the Brooklyn Bridge Animal Welfare Coalition.

And I dedicated this book to my family boyhood cat who lived a long life of 23 years, Sylvia.